The
Climate Conscious
Gardener

Janet Marinelli
Editor

BROOKLYN
BOTANIC
GARDEN

Elizabeth Peters
DIRECTOR OF
PUBLICATIONS

Gerry Moore
SCIENCE EDITOR

Joni Blackburn
COPY EDITOR

Elizabeth Ennis
ART DIRECTOR

Scot Medbury
PRESIDENT

Elizabeth Scholtz
DIRECTOR
EMERITUS

Handbook #195

Copyright © 2010 by Brooklyn Botanic Garden, Inc.

Guides for a Greener Planet are published by
Brooklyn Botanic Garden, 1000 Washington Ave.,
Brooklyn, NY 11225. Visit bbg.org/handbooks.

ISBN 10: 1-889538-49-3
ISBN 13: 978-1-889538-49-5

Printed in China by Ocean Graphics Press.

♻ Printed with soy-based inks on
postconsumer recycled paper.

**Cover: Planting a tree is just one of the many ways gardeners can help offset climate change.
Above: Alpine wildflowers are imperiled by global warming. Rising temperatures are driving
them to higher elevations where it is cooler, but eventually they will have no place to go.**

The Climate Conscious Gardener

A Wake-up Call from the Climate

Janet Marinelli

A few years ago, as I was flying into San Diego for a horticultural conference, I peered out the window as the airplane banked for landing. The sun had set and darkness had fallen, but I could see snaking corridors of flame and huge clouds of sulfurous orange smoke billowing up from below, like a scene from Dante's *Inferno*. Later that evening, scores of area residents took refuge in my hotel from the wildfires, along with their dogs, cats, birds, and what prized possessions they had been able to grab in the rush to evacuate their homes.

The San Diego blazes were part of a series of wildfires that burned across Southern California in October 2007, forcing approximately a million people from their homes—the largest evacuation in the state's history. Nine people died as a direct result of the fires; 85 others were injured; at least 1,500 homes were destroyed; and more than 500,000 acres of landscape were scorched. Among the key factors that contributed to the conflagration was an eight-year-long drought. Data show that global warming has exacerbated the region's natural aridity, and California's fire season, which traditionally extended from June through October, has become a year-round threat.

The effects of climate change, as you'll see in the chapter that follows, are already being felt throughout the United States and around the world. Australia, the Mediterranean region, Kenya, and Brazil as well as parts of North America are enduring epic drought. In the East and Midwest, precipitation patterns are also becoming more extreme, with longer dry spells and heavier downpours. Forests across western North America are succumbing to pests proliferating in the growing heat. Around the globe, spring is arriving earlier. All of this and more is a result of an increase in global mean surface temperature over the last century of *little more than one degree Fahrenheit*. The droughts, fires, and floods of recent years offer a glimpse of what is in store as climate change intensifies. The overwhelming majority of scientists believe that if current trends continue, things will get much worse.

At a September 2009 meeting at the United Nations in New York City, heads of state from around the world were warned by the Intergovernmental Panel on Climate Change, an international group of scientific experts, that greenhouse gas emissions are propelling the planet toward the disastrous impacts described in the panel's worst-case scenarios.

The latest research to come out of the United Kingdom's National Weather Service, which was presented that same month at an international climate conference convened by Oxford University, challenges the assumption that severe warming is a threat only

Sunlight striking the leaves of this Virginia bluebell sets photosynthesis in motion. Via photosynthesis, plants remove carbon dioxide, the major greenhouse gas, from the atmosphere.

for future generations, indicating that without strong action worldwide to curb greenhouse gas emissions, the global mean temperature could rise 7°F by 2060—a few short decades from now. However, the head of the Weather Service, Dr. Richard Betts, emphasized that it's not too late to head off the worst effects. We do have time to avoid the "doomsday scenario," he said, "if we cut greenhouse gas emissions soon." In recent years, the scientific consensus has been that any more than 3.6°F of warming would cause extreme disruption to the planet's natural ecosystems and human communities. According to Weather Service research, to avoid surpassing 3.6°F of warming, currently soaring emissions must peak and start to fall sharply within the next decade.

Gardeners, with their intimate connection to the natural world, have a unique opportunity to demonstrate how to transform concern over climate change into effective action.

In most areas of daily life, whether heating and cooling your home or commuting to work, it is possible to reduce your contribution to climate change, but it's almost impossible, given current technology, to get to carbon neutral, with no net adverse impact on the atmosphere. However, gardeners have the potential to do more than reduce their greenhouse gas emissions! Anyone who has contemplated the process of photosynthesis knows that plants have the marvelous ability to remove carbon dioxide, the leading greenhouse gas, from the atmosphere. Using the sun's energy, they transform CO_2 and water into carbohydrates that fuel plant growth. As plants grow, carbon is stored in their living tissue and remains there over their lifetime, which in many trees can be considerable. This means it is possible to create a garden that is carbon negative—that captures more carbon than it emits in carbon dioxide and its equivalent of other greenhouse gases.

In this book, you'll find step-by-step instructions on how to create such a garden. In "Reducing Your Garden's Climate Footprint," you'll learn about the many ways you can lower your garden's greenhouse gas emissions—from eliminating your use of power tools, which consume fossil fuels and emit carbon dioxide, to minimizing soil cultivation and the use of fertilizers, which increase emissions of carbon dioxide, nitrous oxide, and methane, three powerful greenhouse gases. You'll also learn how to reduce "hidden" carbon emissions that occur during the manufacture and transport of garden products. Actions like these not only make your garden go easier on the atmosphere but also result in less routine maintenance for you.

In "Turning Your Landscape Into a Carbon Sink," you'll discover how your garden can make the most of plants' amazing ability to remove carbon dioxide from the atmosphere and store or "sequester" carbon in their tissues. You'll also learn how to create another kind of horticultural carbon bank by increasing the amount of organic matter in your soil.

What's more, you can use your garden to offset other greenhouse gas emissions. "Landscaping for Home Energy Efficiency" shows how to place trees, shrubs, and

By recording the bloom time of plants such as the California poppy, above, gardeners are helping researchers study the effects of global climate change.

vines strategically to create shade and block blustery winter winds, reducing the amount of energy required to heat and cool your home, and therefore your overall greenhouse gas emissions. "The Climate Footprint of Homegrown Food" describes a number of ways to design and maintain a vegetable garden that minimizes emissions of climate-altering gases and sequesters as much carbon as possible.

Of course, gardening alone can't solve the problem of global climate change. Gardeners manage very little land, so our impact on the atmosphere is small. But that doesn't mean it's insignificant. Understanding the scale of the challenges we will face in our own gardens can help us comprehend the wider implications of climate change for our communities, the country, and the entire planet. This, in turn, can encourage us to make not only our landscapes but also our communities more sustainable, and collectively these actions can have a major impact.

In "Beyond the Garden," you'll learn about a number of different ways gardeners are taking action in their communities—by planting trees, for example, and participating in citizen science projects. We gardeners have always prided ourselves on our intimate knowledge, passed down over generations, about climate, soils, and myriad other interactions that affect our plants. But traditional knowledge about first and last frosts, likely temperatures and precipitation patterns, and the usual timing of pest outbreaks is increasingly unreliable. By participating in citizen science programs such as Project Budburst, gardeners throughout North America are helping researchers understand the effect of global warming on plants and, ultimately, us.

A Gardener's Guide to Climate Change
Janet Marinelli

When gardeners first became aware of climate change, there seemed to be a glimmer of good in the bad news. If global warming meant being able to grow bananas in Albany or heliconias in Kalamazoo, who could complain? As the science has become increasingly clear and the evidence mounts that climate change is not only already here but is happening at a pace almost no one anticipated, however, any positive feelings have turned into apprehension about the sweeping changes under way.

According to the Intergovernmental Panel on Climate Change (IPCC), an international panel of scientists established to assess the risks of global climate change, Earth has already warmed 1.2°F to 1.4°F over the past century. Due to uncertainties about the amount of future greenhouse gas emissions, their net warming effect, and the climate system's response, estimates of future temperature change are educated guesses. With these caveats in mind, the IPCC projected in its 2007 report that the average surface temperature of Earth is likely to increase an additional 2°F to 11.5°F by the end of the 21st century. To put things in perspective, it is only 9°F warmer now than it was during the last ice age.

In the words of the U.S. Global Change Research Program, which coordinates federal research on climate change and in June 2009 published the most comprehensive scientific study to date of global warming and its implications, "It is clear that impacts in the United States are already occurring and are projected to increase in the future, particularly if the concentration of heat-trapping greenhouse gases in the atmosphere continues to rise. So, choices about how we manage greenhouse gas emissions will have far-reaching consequences."

Among the report's key findings:

- **The direct effects of climate change are already evident in the United States, and they are projected to increase.** These include rising temperatures and sea levels, lengthening growing seasons, rapidly retreating glaciers, thawing permafrost, and earlier snowmelt.

- **Climate change is also having secondary impacts on water supplies, agriculture, natural landscapes, and human health.** These impacts differ from region to region and will only grow, according to climate change projections (see "Climate Change, Region by Region," below).

- **Climate change will stress water resources.** With reduced precipitation, increased evaporation, and increased water loss from plants, drought will become

In Georgia, a former farm pond is now parched earth. Global warming has already contributed to record drought in regions around the globe.

an even more serious problem in many regions, especially the West. Declines in mountain snowpack will aggravate water shortages in the West and Alaska.

- **Growers will face increasing challenges.** Although agriculture—and by extension horticulture—is considered one of the economic sectors most adaptable to changes in climate, increased heat, water stress, insect pests, diseases, and weather extremes will require even more versatility.

- **How much climate change we experience in the future, and how disruptive its impacts are, depend on the choices we make today.** The amount of future climate change depends on how well we can control emissions of heat-trapping gases.

Climate Change, Region by Region

The following data from the 2009 U.S. Global Research Program report show that global warming and its related effects are already evident in all major regions of the country, and more of the same is predicted.

Northeast

The annual average temperature in the Northeast has increased by 2°F since 1970, and winter temperatures have risen twice this much. Warming has resulted in many other climate-related changes as well, including more frequent very hot days, a longer growing season, an increase in inundating rains, and less winter precipitation falling as snow and more as rain.

As these trends continue, large portions of the Northeast are likely to become unsuitable for growing popular varieties of apples, blueberries, and cranberries under the worst-case emissions scenarios. The climate conditions suitable for native maple-beech-birch forests are expected to shift dramatically northward, eventually leaving only a small portion of the region with a maple sugar industry, not to mention the colorful fall foliage that is part of the region's iconic character.

Southeast

The annual average temperature in the Southeast has risen 2°F since 1970, with the greatest increase in the winter months. While there has been a 30 percent increase in fall precipitation over most of the region (but a decrease in fall precipitation in southern Florida), summer precipitation has decreased over almost the entire region. Because there has been an increase in heavy downpours, the rain has been falling in fewer events. The net result is that the portion of the Southeast in moderate to severe drought has grown over the past three decades.

Continued warming is projected, with the greatest temperature increases in summer. The higher temperatures and longer periods between rainfall are likely to result in more serious water shortages.

If climate change intensifies, only a small portion of the Northeast is likely to be suitable for traditional crops like cranberries and sugar maple.

Midwest

Average temperatures in the Midwest have risen in recent decades, with the largest increases in winter. The growing season has become longer by one week, mainly due to earlier dates for the last spring frost. Both summer and winter precipitation have been above average for the past three decades, the wettest period in a century. Heavy downpours are now twice as frequent as they were a century ago. The region has experienced two record-breaking floods in the past 15 years.

More frequent, more severe, and longer-lasting heat waves are also projected. The likely shift of precipitation to winter and spring, a larger proportion of heavy downpours, and greater evaporation in summer will mean more floods as well as more summer water shortages. While the longer growing season offers the potential for larger crop yields, farmers and gardeners will be forced to grapple with increases in insects, and weeds, which also thrive with longer periods of warmth.

Great Plains

The average temperature in the Great Plains has already increased roughly 1.5°F since the 1960s and '70s. Relatively cold days are becoming less common and relatively hot days more frequent.

In the southern and central Great Plains, continued increases in summer temperatures are projected to be larger than those in winter. Conditions are expected to become wetter in the north and drier in the southern plains. Also likely are more

Alaskan spruce trees are being killed as spruce bark beetles proliferate and spread northward. Insect pests are also expected to emerge earlier as temperatures continue to rise.

frequent extreme events such as heat waves, droughts, and inundations. Rising temperatures, faster evaporation rates, and more sustained drought will increase the stress on the region's already overdrawn underground water supplies, posing substantial challenges for growers and gardeners, along with insect pests, which are expected to spread northward, emerge earlier, and increase in numbers.

Northwest

Annual average temperature over the region rose about 1.5°F over the past century, and some areas warmed as much as 4°F. Higher temperatures are causing more winter precipitation to fall as rain rather than snow and are contributing to earlier snowmelt.

Further declines in snowpack and earlier spring melt will reduce the amount of water available during the warm season. Higher summer temperatures are expected to increase the risk of forest fires. Drought and warmer temperatures will also increase the frequency and intensity of mountain pine beetle and other insect attacks.

Southwest

Recent warming in the Southwest has been among the most rapid in the country. The temperature increases have made droughts in the region more severe than those of the last several centuries. Record-setting wildfires are resulting from the rising temperatures and related reductions in soil moisture and spring snow cover.

Dramatic warming is expected to continue, and droughts are projected to become even worse, exacerbating the region's already serious water supply problems. Agriculture in the region is likely to suffer, particularly specialty crops in California such as apricots, almonds, artichokes, figs, kiwis, olives, and walnuts, which require a minimum number of hours of winter cold to set fruit for the following year.

Alaska

Over the past 50 years, Alaska has warmed at more than twice the rate of the rest of the United States. Its annual average temperature has increased 3.4°F, and winters have warmed by 6.3°F. The higher temperatures are already causing earlier spring snowmelt, rapid retreat of glaciers, and thawing of the permafrost. Longer summers and higher temperatures are also causing drier conditions. Insect outbreaks and wildfires are increasing—during the 1990s, south-central Alaska experienced the largest outbreak of spruce beetles in the world as rising temperatures allowed the beetle to survive the winter.

Although precipitation may increase, greater evaporation of soil moisture due to higher temperatures is expected to lead to drier conditions overall, meaning farmers and gardeners may not benefit from the longer growing season.

The Impact on Plants

Severe droughts, fierce storms, and rising seas are among the better-known consequences of the global warming already under way. But few gardeners are aware of the implications for plants.

Smoke from the Jesuita wildfire billows up behind Santa Barbara homes in early May 2009. Rising temperatures and resulting reductions in soil moisture are contributing to record-setting blazes.

PLANTS IN PERIL

Following are just a few of the plants that studies suggest are threatened by climate change.

Bluebells The English bluebell, *Hyacinthoides non-scripta*, is a spring-flowering bulb with fragrant bell-shaped flowers that stand upright when they are in bud but hang downwards, nodding in the breeze, when fully open. For thousands of years, its ability to store food underground in its bulbs has enabled the English bluebell to get off to an early start in spring. With the warmer springs induced by climate change, English bluebells, already globally threatened, will lose this advantage and could be outcompeted by other plants able to start growing earlier than in the past.

Eastern Prairie White-Fringed Orchid In late June and early July, this exquisite wild orchid, known botanically as *Platanthera leucophaea*, produces a spike composed of 5 to 40 white flowers, each with a spectacular three-part fringed lower petal about an inch long and a one- to two-inch-long nectar spur that hangs below. Loss of its tallgrass prairie habitat, primarily in northeastern Illinois, the disappearance of its hawk moth pollinator, and competition by invasive species have all already put the orchid on the federal endangered species list. As the local climate dries and warms, the species could become extinct in the wild.

Cyclamens Found naturally throughout the Mediterranean except for Spain and Egypt, members of the genus *Cyclamen* are beloved for their heart- or kidney-

shaped and often patterned leaves and elegant flowers in shades of pink, purple, red, and white with petals bent back 180 degrees. In a 2006 study, researchers found that the distinct climate niches favored by cyclamens will become increasingly rare and may be gone by the 2050s. Some species are adaptable enough and could survive climate change, but many will probably disappear in the wild.

The eastern prairie white-fringed orchid, a native plant already on the federal endangered list, will struggle to maintain its range in the face of climate change.

Plants and animals are moving in response to global warming, all at their own pace. Migrating pollinators like the monarch butterfly could find themselves without their favored nectar sources.

Boston University biology professor Richard Primack and researcher Abraham Miller-Rushing retraced the footsteps of Henry David Thoreau to determine how the birches, blueberries, goldenrods, and other wildflowers of the historic Concord, Massachusetts, landscape once frequented by the famous naturalist have been faring. They discovered that from 1852 to 2006, due to a combination of urbanization and climate change, Concord has warmed 4.3°F. As a result, plants are flowering seven days earlier, on average, than they did in Thoreau's day. Other studies have demonstrated that spring is coming earlier by about a week not just in Concord but around the globe.

As a result of global warming, plants are already on the move. Climate change has forced plants and animals throughout the Northern Hemisphere to scurry an average of 3.7 miles per decade toward the poles and almost 20 feet per decade up mountainsides. Camphor weed (*Heterotheca subaxillaris*), for example, a wildflower in the aster family with late-summer yellow daisylike flowers and leaves that smell like camphor when crushed, is a southern United States species that has been spreading northward. In his 1915 *Flora of the Vicinity of New York*, Norman Taylor described camphor weed as "scarcely persistent." Today, says Gerry Moore, director of science at Brooklyn Botanic Garden, it is common in sandy open sites throughout the New York metropolitan area, especially along the coast.

To keep pace with global warming, some plants will be forced to shift their ranges hundreds of miles northward. Countless species will not be able to migrate

THE ZONE MAP FLAP

Who would have thought that the humble hardiness zone map would become the most contentious issue in American horticulture since the debate over using native versus exotic plants?

Hardiness zone maps are the basic tools gardeners have used for decades to determine if a particular plant can survive winter in their area. The best-known plant hardiness zone map, produced by the U.S. Department of Agriculture (USDA), divides the country into 11 color-coded bands or zones according to average annual minimum temperature, based on the lowest temperatures recorded for the 13 years from 1974 to 1986 in the United States and Canada and from 1971 to 1984 in Mexico. Each successive zone represents a 10°F difference in the average annual minimum temperature—the higher the number, the warmer the temperatures for gardening in that zone.

The labels on most plants for sale at nurseries include their hardiness zone, almost invariably based on the USDA map. However, this map, which was last published in 1990, is now badly out of date, because it doesn't account for the significant warming we've experienced in the past couple of decades.

Several years ago, the American Horticultural Society produced an updated map for the USDA, based on 16 years' worth of more recent weather data. But the USDA rejected the map and went back to the drawing board, producing in-house a map based on 30 years of weather records—in effect minimizing the evidence of recent warming. Hence the controversy: Critics say that at worst the still-to-be-released map reflects an attempt to bury evidence of global warming, and at best it renders the map unreliable for gardeners, since plants don't care what the climate was like 30 years ago but rather thrive or fail based on the climate now.

The Arbor Day Foundation stepped in to fill the breach. In 2006, using the same basic zone structure as the USDA, it produced a map based on a 15-year set of recent weather data similar to that used for the American Horticultural Society map rejected by the USDA. In a press release announcing the release of its new map, the Arbor Day Foundation noted that it "reflects that many areas have become warmer since 1990 when the last USDA hardiness zone map was published. Significant portions of many states have shifted at least one full hardiness zone…. Some areas around the country have even warmed two full zones."

To emphasize the point, the foundation even provided a feature on its website that illustrates the warming that has occurred (arborday.org/media/mapchanges). A computer-animated map redraws the old 1990 USDA hardiness zones to reflect the latest data, showing dramatically how the zones have shifted northward.

Differences Between 1990 USDA Hardiness Zones and 2006 Arbor Day Foundation Hardiness Zones

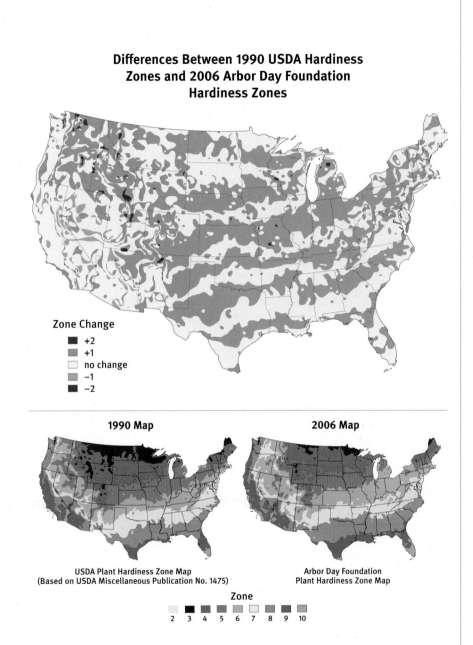

Zone Change
- ■ +2
- ▨ +1
- □ no change
- ▨ −1
- ■ −2

1990 Map

2006 Map

USDA Plant Hardiness Zone Map
(Based on USDA Miscellaneous Publication No. 1475)

Arbor Day Foundation
Plant Hardiness Zone Map

Zone
2 3 4 5 6 7 8 9 10

The bloom time of many plants, like forest phlox (*Phlox divaricata*), is changing as spring arrives earlier.

fast enough, and others will be stopped dead in their tracks by housing subdivisions, shopping malls, and sprawling industrial complexes. Recent studies predict that climate change could result in the extinction of up to half of the world's plant species by the end of the century (see "Plants in Peril," page 14).

What's more, once-familiar natural landscapes are likely to change drastically in the decades to come. Plants and the pollinators and other animals that depend on them, all moving at their own pace, will find themselves with implausible companions. In a hundred years, California's Central Valley, for example, could be the preferred habitat for cacti and succulents now found in Arizona. Along the coast, California's iconic redwoods could still be hanging on because adult trees are so long-lived. But they will be a forest of the "living dead," unable to reproduce. Scientists have only recently begun to consider the ramifications of a not-too-distant future when there may be no redwoods in California and no sugar maples in Vermont.

This is staggering news for conservationists, whose work is already made difficult by the rapid destruction of habitat and its invasion by aggressive nonnative species. They are being forced to reexamine even the most basic assumptions. "How do we define 'native'?" asks Gwen Stauffer, former director of the New England Wild Flower Society, as plants from the South move northward into the region. "What is a natural community? And how do we decide which plants deserve protection?"

Climate change is also making life increasingly complicated for gardeners. Hardiness zone maps, the tried-and-true method of figuring out what plants will survive in an area, have become a matter of debate as temperatures have warmed (see "The Zone Map Flap," page 16). Other traditional horticultural practices are also being called into question as pests expand their ranges northward with rising temperatures, there are more generations of some insect pests per year, and precipitation patterns become increasingly extreme, with both longer droughts and more deluges. However, horticultural research on the most effective responses has barely begun, at least in the United States.

Good-bye English Cottage Garden?

The British are light-years ahead in assessing the effects of climate change on gardeners. In this nation famous for its love of gardens and impressive 500-year horticultural history, a coalition of high-powered groups, including the Royal Horticultural Society, Royal Botanic Gardens, Kew, and the National Trust, which preserves historic houses and gardens, funded the 2002 study "Gardening in the Global Greenhouse: The Impacts of Climate Change on Gardens in the U.K." One of the study's astonishing conclusions is that climate change could bring about rapid changes in garden style. For example, as climate change intensifies, the English cottage garden as we know it will become difficult to maintain—and could even become a thing of the past.

The report painstakingly lays out the likely effects of climate change in the British Isles on everything from temperatures (higher), rainfall (less, falling with greater intensity when it does occur), and insect pests and diseases (more of both). Summers will be hotter and drier, a particular problem for gardeners in parts of southern England where water is already in short supply, and winters will be warmer and wetter. Traditional herbaceous border plants like delphinium and phlox will not adapt well to drier summers, and old cultivars of iris, which are killed by waterlogged soils in winter, will also require intensive care. More thorough staking will be necessary to prevent herbaceous plants from getting pelted down during downpours.

According to the study, intrepid British gardeners will likely be replacing their phlox and delphiniums with bananas and bamboos in the decades ahead. It also

Sustaining the character and plant combinations of some traditional landscape styles, such as the English cottage garden, will become increasingly difficult as weather patterns alter.

As a result of burning fossil fuels and other human activities during the past century, atmospheric levels of carbon dioxide are higher than they have been in the past 650,000 years.

predicts that there will be new marketing opportunities for environmentally benign solutions such as composting and other organic gardening techniques, water storage equipment, and biological control methods for managing pests.

Global Warming Basics

It's time to dust off the old environmental catchphrase "Think globally, act locally." Everything we do in our gardens is tied into fundamental processes that govern life on Earth, and in order to reduce our contribution to climate change we need to understand what these are and how they work.

The Greenhouse Effect

By now we've all heard the term "greenhouse effect." Especially to us gardeners, it once evoked warm images of glasshouses brimming with beautiful plants, but no longer. In our age of climate change it has increasingly serious implications for the health of gardens and natural landscapes alike. If you understand the greenhouse effect, you have a pretty good idea of what's going on with the global climate.

Energy from the sun drives the planet's climate and weather. Earth absorbs energy from the sun and also radiates some back into space. Anyone who's been inside a greenhouse on a sunny day knows that it can really heat up. Much like the glass of a greenhouse, gases in the atmosphere trap the sun's heat. The gases allow the sun's rays to pass through and warm the planet—in fact, without this natural greenhouse effect, temperatures would be about 60°F lower than they are now, and life as we know it would not be possible. But these so-called greenhouse gases also prevent heat from escaping the atmosphere into space.

For thousands of years, the levels of greenhouse gases in the atmosphere—mainly water vapor, carbon dioxide, methane, and nitrous oxide—remained essentially stable. Natural processes removed as much of the gases as they released (see "A Gardener's Guide to the Carbon Cycle" and "A Gardener's Guide to the Nitrogen Cycle," pages 24 and 27). But during the past century or so, human activities, especially the burning of oil, coal, and other fossil fuels, deforestation, and intensive agriculture, have added huge quantities of carbon dioxide and other natural greenhouse gases. We've also added some heat-trapping industrial chemicals to the mix, making things even worse. Atmospheric levels of both carbon dioxide and methane are the highest they've been in the past 650,000 years. These added gases are enhancing the natural greenhouse effect, and the vast majority of climate scientists believe they are responsible for the increase in global average temperature and related climate changes that have occurred.

The Major Greenhouse Gases

The Kyoto Protocol, the international agreement to address climate change, was adopted in 1997 and as of November 2009 had been signed and ratified by 187 countries; the United States is not one of them. The protocol covers three major greenhouse gases—carbon dioxide, methane, and nitrous oxide—as well as three classes of industrial chemicals—hydrofluorocarbons, perfluorocarbons, and sulphur hexafluoride. Carbon dioxide, methane, and nitrous oxide are also the gases most intimately connected with the act of gardening.

Carbon dioxide (CO_2) Carbon dioxide is a seemingly innocuous gas that occurs naturally in the atmosphere as part of one of the planet's fundamental natural processes, the carbon cycle (see page 24). However, it is becoming disproportionately abundant as we burn fossil fuels for energy and chop down forests. Scientists believe that global climate change is

Clear-cutting reduces the landscape's ability to absorb carbon dioxide.

HOW LOW SHOULD WE GO?

What level of greenhouse gases in the atmosphere should we be shooting for? This has been a vexing—and politically charged—question.

Although carbon dioxide is not the most powerful greenhouse gas, it's by far the most common and significant of those generated by humans, and for this reason greenhouse gas targets are often expressed in parts per million of CO_2. For millions of years, the concentration of CO_2 in the atmosphere hovered under 300 ppm (parts per million by volume), but by 2009 it was approaching 400 ppm. The level deemed "safe"—above which the resulting temperature rise and other climate changes will likely cause extreme disruption to the planet's ecological and social systems—has been a moving target. The consensus settled at 450 ppm, which until recently most scientists believed would raise world temperatures above preindustrial levels by 3.6°F. Based on current scientific findings, the author Bill McKibben, along with some leading climate scientists such as James Hansen of the National Aeronautics and Space Administration, have launched a campaign to convince policymakers and the public that if we allow concentrations to reach 450 ppm, we risk reaching tipping points and irreversible impacts, such as the melting of the planet's permafrost, which would result in major methane releases.

What is happening in the Arctic, they say, is evidence that climate change is occurring much faster than expected. In the summer of 2007, sea ice was roughly 39 percent below the summer average for 1979 to 2000, and researchers now believe that the Arctic could be completely ice free by 2011 to 2015—80 years ahead of what they had predicted just a few short years ago. For this reason, many now believe that the highest safe level of carbon dioxide is 350 ppm, a much more ambitious goal but one that will more likely lead to a future climate that resembles our current one.

Melting permafrost causes trees to tumble, creating "drunken forests" like this one in Fairbanks, Alaska, and releases methane into the atmosphere.

Wetlands are a natural source of methane, but it is estimated that two-thirds of the emissions of this powerful greenhouse gas are from man-made sources like livestock farms and landfills.

caused primarily by this greenhouse gas—according to an analysis of greenhouse gas emissions in 2004, CO_2 accounted for almost 77 percent of the heat-trapping potential caused by human activities.

Atmospheric CO_2 concentrations have increased from approximately 280 parts per million (ppm) in preindustrial times to 390 ppm in the early 21st century—almost a 40 percent increase. (Parts per million is a common unit of measurement used to express the concentration of a substance within air or other gases, liquids, or solids.) According to the IPCC, almost all of the increase is from man-made sources. If emissions continue at the current rate, carbon dioxide concentrations will be 609 ppm by the end of the century.

Methane (CH_4) Methane emissions are small compared with carbon dioxide, but the gas has 21 times the heat-trapping potential of CO_2.

Methane is formed naturally when plants decay where there is very little air. It is often called swamp gas because it's so abundant around marshes and other wetlands. Human activities also release a significant amount of methane into the atmosphere. In fact, it's estimated that today, almost two-thirds of global methane emissions are caused by humans. In the United States, the largest methane emissions come from the decomposition of waste in landfills, livestock farming, natural gas and oil production, and coal mining.

Methane concentrations increased sharply during most of the 20th century, and by the early 21st century were 150 percent above preindustrial levels.

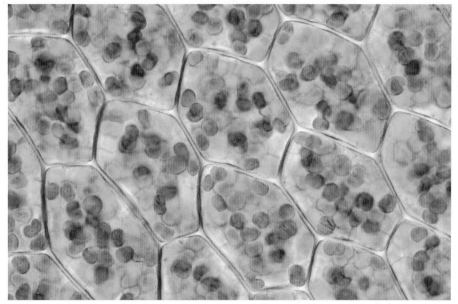

Plants are the foundation of the biological carbon cycle. In plant-cell chloroplasts like these, the sun's energy is used to transform CO_2 and water into sugars and other carbon compounds.

Nitrous Oxide (N_2O) Carbon dioxide and methane have been receiving the most attention, but nitrous oxide ranks right up there as a cause of concern because of its heat-trapping ability—300 times more per molecule than CO_2.

Best known as the anesthetic "laughing gas," nitrous oxide occurs naturally in the atmosphere in minute amounts as part of the nitrogen cycle (see page 27). Just as with carbon dioxide and methane, however, we've been responsible for increasing the levels of nitrous oxide in the atmosphere. Agricultural practices are a big part of the reason why. Natural emissions of nitrous oxide in soils are increased by a variety of agricultural and horticultural activities, such as the use of synthetic and organic fertilizers and even soil cultivation.

Nitrous oxide has increased approximately 18 percent in the past 200 years.

A Gardener's Guide to the Carbon Cycle

The three greenhouse gases of greatest concern, carbon dioxide, methane, and nitrous oxide, are tied into two fundamental processes, the carbon cycle and the nitrogen cycle. Technically known as biogeochemical cycles, they constantly recycle chemicals that are vital to life. Every time we gardeners plant, fertilize, or compost, we're intervening in these processes, and by adjusting how we go about such basic horticultural practices we can minimize our generation of these climate-altering gases.

Carbon, the chemical element represented by the symbol C, is the building block of life on Earth. The fourth most abundant chemical element in the universe by mass, carbon has an affinity for bonding with other atoms and forms an extraordinary variety of compounds, including carbon dioxide (one carbon atom bonded to two oxygen atoms, or CO_2) and methane (one carbon atom bonded to four hydrogen atoms, or CH_4).

As part of the carbon cycle, this element is constantly moving between the atmosphere, the oceans, sedimentary rocks, soil, plants, and animals over both short and long time frames. The geological or nonliving carbon cycle takes place over hundreds of millions of years as large amounts of the element sink to the ocean floor and become buried in Earth's crust, where it may remain for eons until a volcanic eruption or other geological event spews it back into the atmosphere. By contrast, the biological carbon cycle occurs over days, weeks, months, or years as plants and animals go about the business of life.

Plants are the foundation of the biological carbon cycle. Via photosynthesis they have the amazing ability to pluck sunlight out of thin air and use its energy to convert carbon dioxide and water into complex carbohydrates, the building blocks of the foods that all animals, including us, need to survive. As a result, carbon is a big part of the living tissue that plants and animals are made of, their biomass. We're urged to plant trees as a way to fight global warming because as they grow, trees absorb significant amounts of carbon dioxide. The carbon is locked up in their tissues over their lifetime, which in many species can be considerable.

The cycle continues when plants and animals die and the carbon in their tissues becomes food for the microbes, called decomposers, that feast on their remains. As

When plants die and decompose, some of the carbon stored in their tissues over their lifetime is released back into the atmosphere in the form of carbon dioxide.

any compost enthusiast knows, when the appropriate mixture of carbon-rich materials like dry leaves and nitrogen-rich materials such as grass clippings are combined and moisture and oxygen are provided, these decomposers produce a humus-rich soil amendment that enriches garden soil. In the process, they also release some carbon dioxide back into the atmosphere. However, if too much water is provided, anaerobic bacteria, which can decompose organic tissue without oxygen, take over. Anyone who has added too much water to a compost pile knows all too well that among the byproducts of anaerobic decomposition are ammonia and methane, which smell awful. The same anaerobic process occurs naturally in habitats with saturated soils, such as marshes and swamps.

Sometimes plant and animal remains are buried in the earth or sink to the ocean floor, beyond the reach of the decomposers. Over hundreds of millions of years, they are subject to forces such as high temperature and geologic pressure and become hydrocarbons—long chains of carbon atoms bound to each other and to hydrogen atoms—also known as fossil fuels. This is how the planet's vast coal deposits, for example, were created. Coal formed from the dead remains of enormous tree ferns, colossal lycopods, and huge horsetails, the ancient relatives of modern club mosses and horsetails, as well as odd-looking early conifers called *Cordaites* with long, strap-like leaves—all of which thrived in the warm and humid swamp forests of the Carboniferous period, 360 to 286 million years ago.

For millennia, tropical forests have served as vast carbon reservoirs. When they are cleared, often by burning, much of the carbon stored in the trees is released directly as CO_2.

It took hundreds of millions of years to trap all this carbon deep in the earth and under the ocean floor. But by extracting and burning it, we've managed to release much of it back into the atmosphere in a couple of centuries. Carbon dioxide is a by-product of burning these carbon-rich fuels—whether in a power plant, a car, a lawnmower, or a leaf blower—and now the atmosphere is overflowing with the carbon that had been locked up in these ancient deposits of coal and other fossil fuels.

We've also altered the biological carbon cycle, increasing atmospheric CO_2 levels still further through activities like forest clearing and farming. When forests are cleared, often in the tropics through the use of fire, much of the carbon stored in the trees is released directly into the air as CO_2.

Agriculture has largely depleted the organic matter in soil, once a huge storehouse of carbon.

Clearing the land eliminates the trees, which would otherwise remove massive amounts of carbon from the air via photosynthesis. The plants, which are CO_2 consumers, are replaced by people, CO_2 producers.

A great deal of carbon in the form of organic matter was once stored in the soil. Other than carbonate rocks, soils are believed to be the largest terrestrial storehouse of carbon (see "Carbon Sequestration in Soil," page 80). However, agriculture has largely depleted the soils of organic matter, resulting in even more CO_2 in the atmosphere.

A Gardener's Guide to the Nitrogen Cycle

While carbon dioxide and methane are players in the carbon cycle, nitrous oxide, the third most worrisome greenhouse gas, is involved in the nitrogen cycle. Nitrogen is constantly cycling back and forth in various forms between the atmosphere and the soil. As gardeners know, nitrogen is the nutrient needed in the largest amount by plants, and managing nitrogen in the soil is a key part of growing a healthy and productive garden.

Almost 80 percent of Earth's atmosphere is composed of elemental nitrogen, or N_2. In this elemental form, nitrogen is fairly inert and has no appreciable effect on global warming. The elemental nitrogen is constantly being taken out of the atmosphere by microorganisms in the soil and converted to forms like ammonium and nitrates that plants can use, a process called nitrogen fixation. Some nitrogen-fixing bacteria, such as *Rhizobium*, live in the root nodules of legumes like peas and beans, alfalfa, and clover in a symbiotic relationship: The plants supply the bacteria with energy and nutrients and in return have what amounts to their own, built-in nitrogen factories. Many organic gardeners grow these plants as cover crops to help ensure a good level of nitrogen in their soil.

Other microbes carry on a reverse process called denitrification, which converts the fixed nitrogen in the soil into elemental nitrogen and nitrous oxide. Supplementing the soil's nitrogen supply with either synthetic or organic nitrogen fertilizers increases the natural process of denitrification and therefore nitrous oxide emissions. In fact, soils enriched with nitrogen fertilizer emit two to ten times as much nitrous oxide as unfertilized soils.

Carbon Sources and Carbon Sinks

A garden can be either a carbon source or a carbon sink. A carbon source is one that emits more carbon dioxide than it absorbs. Conversely, a carbon sink absorbs more carbon dioxide than it emits.

Carbon sources can be either natural or man-made. When you burn fossil fuels to mow your lawn or power a rototiller, you are creating a man-made carbon source. One of the largest natural sources of atmospheric carbon dioxide is the decomposition of dead plant and animal tissue by microorganisms. In other words, composting can be a source of carbon emissions in the garden too (see "The Composting Controversy," page 44).

The oceans are among the planet's greatest natural carbon sinks. As we've seen, so are forests, since during the process of photosynthesis, trees absorb CO_2 and store elemental carbon in their tissue. Earth's soils also represent a huge reservoir of carbon in the form of plant litter and other biomass that accumulates as organic matter. In fact, soils are believed to contain more carbon than all terrestrial vegetation and the atmosphere combined. So by growing trees and increasing the organic matter content of your soils, you increase your garden's ability to be a carbon sink and "sequester" carbon, the technical term for the process by which carbon sinks capture and store carbon dioxide from the atmosphere.

Carbon Neutral and Carbon Negative

The popular term for the total greenhouse gas emissions caused directly or indirectly by an individual, an organization, a geographic area such as a garden or a nation, or a particular product is "carbon footprint." The term is often used to express not only the amount of carbon dioxide that may be released but also its equivalent of other greenhouse gases emitted, such as methane and nitrous oxide. The carbon dioxide

It is possible to create a carbon-negative garden by reducing greenhouse gas emissions and making the most of soil's and plants' ability to store carbon.

equivalent of methane, for example, is computed by multiplying the amount of the gas emitted, in weight, by its global warming potential of 21 (methane has 21 times more heat-trapping ability per molecule than CO_2). For clarity, we use the term "climate footprint" instead of "carbon footprint" in this handbook when discussing carbon equivalence.

When a garden has no adverse climate footprint, it is described as "carbon neutral." For gardeners, being carbon neutral means balancing the amount of greenhouse gases caused directly or indirectly by your landscape with an equivalent amount of carbon sequestration. However, gardeners have the potential not only to make their activities less harmful but to actually make the situation better. If you reduce your emissions enough and sequester enough carbon in your plants and soil, theoretically you can reach the pinnacle of horticultural climate mitigation—a carbon-negative garden.

Reducing Your Garden's Climate Footprint

Janet Marinelli

Doug Kent is a pioneer of climate-friendly landscaping. He's also a bit of an iconoclast. "Gardeners think green is good," Kent says as he ushers me around one of his gardens in Manhattan Beach, California. Because growing plants is the essence of gardening, and the plants pull carbon dioxide from the atmosphere in the process of photosynthesis, we figure our landscapes must be beneficial in an age of climate change caused mostly by this greenhouse gas. But the reality is that almost all gardens are a source of CO_2—often a lot of it. Kent has demonstrated, however, that it is possible to create landscapes that go easy on the atmosphere.

The Manhattan Beach garden is a prime example, though at first glance you wouldn't know it. Like many suburban yards it has several shade trees, including an impressive California sycamore (*Platanus racemosa*) that casts a leafy canopy over much of the backyard. California flannelbush (*Fremontodendron californicum*), golden monkey flower (*Mimulus guttatus*), and fuschsia-flowering gooseberry (*Ribes speciosum*) are just a few of the native wildflowers that attract butterflies and hummingbirds. A little bird garden with a trickling fountain is tucked in one corner of the backyard. The landscape even has a full-size bocce ball court, as well as a collection of recycled garden ornaments, including an old phone booth.

What the garden does not have is lawn, the cause of myriad environmental problems due to the amount of energy consumed and pollution emitted by mowers and other power tools, water used for irrigation, and synthetic fertilizers and pesticides commonly applied to turf. The landscape's mostly native and Mediterranean plants require very little water and no chemical pesticides or fertilizers—only homemade compost.

For the past 60 years, fossil fuels have become the lifeblood of the American garden, as for the economy as a whole. Look closely and it's not difficult to see how the amount of energy used to maintain the typical garden results in a surprisingly large amount of carbon dioxide and other greenhouse gas emissions. For starters, we consume energy directly, by deploying the entire panoply of power equipment deemed essential for a proper modern landscape, from mowers and blowers to weed whackers. The energy involved in pumping and distributing the water we use for irrigation can be another major source of CO_2; generally, the more arid the area, the higher the water's "embodied energy," the technical term for this indirect form of energy consumption. The fertilizers and pesticides with which we routinely coddle our gardens account for still more energy consumption and greenhouse gas

Reducing a garden's climate footprint begins with slashing energy consumption. One lovely alternative to high-input conventional lawn in the East is foam flower and creeping phlox.

Landscape construction can have a major climate footprint. Careful design and material selection can minimize a garden's impact on the atmosphere.

emissions. The manufacture of synthetic fertilizer, made mostly from natural gas, is extremely energy intensive. Chemical pesticides also have high embodied energy, and they're toxic to boot.

This reliance on fossil fuels creates a kind of vicious circle. We force-feed our plants with chemical fertilizers and water like crazy to make them grow, grow, grow. Then we burn fossil fuels to power the mowers and clippers we need to keep the grass and shrubs under control. The clippings typically are hauled away to a landfill instead of composted and used to return organic matter and nutrients to the soil. As a result, we need to apply even more fertilizer to keep things growing.

Garden maintenance is just one part of the problem. Garden construction also has a major impact on the atmosphere. Construction can be so energy intensive that it may take many years to offset the CO_2 emissions. Paving surfaces represent an especially large amount of embodied energy. Throw in planters, fences, fountains, garden furniture, and the other accoutrements of a well-appointed landscape, and the emissions really pile up.

The good news is that although a garden that goes easy on the atmosphere requires changing a 60-year-old mind-set and some by-now routine practices, ultimately it is both better for the environment and less trouble to maintain.

Carbon Calculators
Before you can begin reducing its impact on the atmosphere, you need to determine what your garden's major sources of greenhouse gas emissions are. This in turn will

A CHECKLIST FOR GARDEN CONSTRUCTION AND RENOVATION

With careful planning you can not only substantially reduce the greenhouse gas emissions associated with landscape installation and materials but also create a garden that will continue to minimize your impact on the atmosphere for many years to come. Here are some things to consider:

☐ Protect as much healthy natural landscape as possible, especially actively growing trees.

☐ Preserve and restore the soil. Protect healthy soils from damage by construction equipment and other disturbance. Restore the carbon content of degraded soils with compost.

☐ Locate trees, shrubs, and windbreaks where they will block winter winds and provide shade in summer. This will reduce the amount of energy required to heat and cool your home and thus reduce your overall climate footprint.

☐ Drastically limit the size of turf areas. Better yet, eliminate lawn entirely. Instead, create decks or patios for living space, and enlarge planting beds.

☐ To capture as much carbon as possible, maximize the planting area in the landscape and minimize the pavement. For example, a driveway comprised of two ribbons of pavement with groundcovers in the middle is better than one that is totally blacktopped.

☐ Woody plants capture more carbon than fleshy herbaceous species, so plant as much of your property as possible with trees and shrubs, preferably native species that also provide food and habitat for birds and other wildlife. Prairies can be very productive ecosystems and capture a lot of carbon, and thus they are suitable models for the regions in which they are the predominant plant community.

☐ Select drought-tolerant plants for your landscape, ideally those that can also tolerate periods of saturation, since with climate change, many regions will be experiencing rainstorms that are less frequent but more intense.

☐ Incorporate any existing materials on the site into your garden design. If additional materials are required, choose ones salvaged from other nearby locations and those with the lowest embodied energy—brick and concrete have large carbon footprints compared to, say, wood.

☐ Buy plants and other products that have been produced locally and ideally have been certified by an independent organization to meet a set of rigorous standards designed to minimize global climate change.

☐ Make room for homegrown food.

You'll find additional information on how to accomplish these goals throughout this handbook.

reveal the most effective courses of action. The most popular way to determine your overall climate footprint is to use a carbon calculator. As more and more people have become aware of climate change and the role they can play in reducing their own impact, these interactive web tools have been proliferating like rabbits.

One of the most widely used is the EPA's Household Emissions Calculator. Its format is typical: You follow simple instructions, typing personal information into boxes—the number of people in your household, how many cars you have and how many miles you drive on average, how much fossil fuel you use in your house each month, how much you recycle, and so on. The computer then calculates your carbon emissions in each category.

There are also more specific carbon calculators that can tell you whether the greener breakfast choice is, say, scrambled eggs or steel-cut oats. There is an office paper calculator that helps you figure out the number of trees used for your company's latest annual report, shows the environmental impact of different papers, and offers carbon-cutting strategies for using less paper and choosing paper with a higher percentage of recycled content. There are also calculators that help you determine the greenhouse gas emissions resulting from air travel.

What there is not, at least not yet, is a carbon calculator for gardeners. At this point, the closest thing we have is Build Carbon Neutral (www.buildcarbonneutral.com/), a carbon calculator developed by the Lady Bird Johnson Wildflower Center and the design firm Mithun. Build Carbon Neutral enables professionals and homeowners to design an entire site, building and landscape, to reduce its carbon emissions. Unlike most similar carbon calculators, which estimate the CO_2 released during the day-to-day operation of buildings, this one calculates the total amount of carbon dioxide produced as a result of the energy required to manufacture, transport, and assemble construction materials. Other calculators also fail to account for the carbon held in vegetation and soils, sometimes for hundreds of years. Build Carbon Neutral takes into account not only the size of the project and the materials used to build it, but also the eco-region in which it is located, the amount and type of landscape removed, and the amount and type of landscape added. In other words, it estimates the amount of CO_2 sequestered or released as a result of the destruction or restoration of natural vegetation, such as prairie or forest.

We do not yet have a calculator that can estimate the climate footprint of garden construction and maintenance as well as the landscape's ability to offset emissions and sequester carbon. In the meantime, you can be confident that taking the following steps will dramatically reduce your landscape's greenhouse gas emissions.

Retire the Power Tools

Next time you're in the garden department of a well-stocked chain store, take a look at the plethora of power tools for sale. There will undoubtedly be push mowers,

Power tools consume fossil fuels and collectively release considerable carbon dioxide. Using reel mowers and other hand tools saves money and minimizes greenhouse gas emissions.

riding mowers, leaf blowers, lawn edgers and trenchers, hedge trimmers, weed whackers, chippers, shredders, rototillers, chain saws, string trimmers, power seeders and spreaders, pumps, power sprayers—the variety of power tools is mind-boggling. Whether they run on gas or are powered by electricity, these tools collectively result in significant carbon dioxide emissions.

How smitten are we with our gardening machines? According to the EPA, we clock in more than three billion hours a year using gas-powered lawn and garden equipment alone. The agency also estimates that operating a lawn mower for just one hour emits as much pollution as driving a car about 20 miles.

Things are getting better. More and more people are swapping gas-powered models for energy-efficient—and quiet—electric ones, and old-fashioned motorless reel mowers are making a comeback. New technology is being developed all the time, including the new breed of battery- and solar-powered robotic mowers, which zigzag across the lawn, cutting work time and emissions along with the grass. Even these high-tech helpers are not free of a carbon footprint, however—there are still embodied energy and greenhouse gas emissions associated with the materials they're made of and the fuel required for their manufacture.

The best way to minimize CO_2 emissions is to retire the power tools and use hand tools whenever possible instead. If you reduce the size of your lawn, you won't need much more than a reel mower. And if you avoid formal hedges and other manicured landscape features, you can retire the power trimmers along with the power mower.

Some studies suggest that lawn can sequester a lot of carbon. But other plantings can function as carbon sinks without causing the numerous environmental problems associated with turf.

Rethink the Lawn

I've never understood the American romance with the lawn. In my mind, it's hard to fall in love with a grass plant when its identity has been subsumed in a lawn, the horticultural equivalent of a Stalinist collective. So why is it grass that has become the official symbol of suburbia, the heart of the American view of the ideal life? Not the kitchen garden, as in Italy. Not the flower border, as in England. Turfgrass. Go figure.

According to the Turf Institute, there are an estimated 46.5 million acres of turfgrass in the United States alone—an area greater than the states of Pennsylvania, Delaware, and Rhode Island combined. Some recent research suggests that all this lawn can sequester significant amounts of carbon. To capture the maximum amount of carbon, according to the studies, the turf must be fertilized, irrigated, and mowed to keep the grass growing and actively pulling carbon dioxide from the atmosphere. Given the numerous environmental problems associated with lawn maintenance, however, as well as the fact that there are other, more diversity-friendly ways to store carbon, the trade-off hardly seems worthwhile.

In their book *Redesigning the American Lawn*, F. Herbert Bormann, Diana Balmori, and Gordon T. Geballe marshal an impressive list of statistics on the annual environmental and economic costs of turfgrass: 580 million gallons of gasoline are used by lawn mowers, for example. As much as $5.25 billion is spent on fertilizers derived from fossil fuels, and an additional $700 million is spent on the poisons used to kill grubs and other turfgrass pests. A NASA scientist estimated that turfgrass

BE A PLANT MOVER

Studies indicate that plants and animals will be forced to rapidly shift their ranges for the next century or two to keep pace with climate change. Many won't be able to make it on their own. This has led some scientists to speculate that gardeners and other plant enthusiasts will need to lend a helping hand. In fact, we already are.

In a study published in the Ecological Society of America journal *Frontiers in Ecology and Environment*, five biologists looked into whether commercial nurseries and gardeners in Europe may be providing a head start for some plants. They found that 73 percent of the 357 native European plant species they investigated are being sold hundreds or even thousands of kilometers north of their natural geographic range limits, where climate change is expected to create suitable habitat in the future. Their conclusion: We're already assisting plants to migrate northward, even if unwittingly. "In some cases, they write," this may allow extinction to be averted."

To what extent humans should intervene to prevent extinctions by moving species north or wherever conditions are suitable—called assisted migration or managed relocation—has become one of the hottest debates in contemporary conservation biology, due to concern that moving plants well beyond their natural ranges could cause some species to become invasive. And even if invasion were not a risk, horticulture would not be a solution for all species, since gardeners tend to favor only plants with showy leaves or flowers. In fact, the 260 species in the study that were expanding their range thanks to commercial nurseries represent a relatively small fraction of the European flora, and members of the mint, aster, buttercup, and rose family were disproportionately represented.

While biologists debate the safety of assisted migration, however, there are relatively safe steps gardeners can take to help some plants shift their ranges in response to global warming. It's especially important to choose long-lived woody plants carefully, as they're most likely to experience substantial climate change over their lifetimes. For example, if you live in southern New York State and you're shopping around for a red maple (*Acer rubrum*), which is native throughout the eastern half of the United States from Florida and Texas north into Canada, it makes sense to look for a specimen that has been propagated from trees growing well south of your garden, which are better adapted to a warmer climate.

Information on the provenance, or origin, of plants isn't readily available in plant catalogs or on labels, so make a point of asking. What's more, because the overwhelming majority of invasive plants are not native to the biome, or regional ecosystem, there's relatively little risk for a southern New York gardener to grow a more southerly species such as large fothergilla (*Fothergilla major*), one of the most beautiful shrubs of the southern Appalachians, with bottlebrush-like flower spikes that exude a rich honey scent in spring.

is the single largest irrigated crop in the United States, and the water required to sustain it is substantial. According to the EPA, in the East, 30 percent of municipal water is lavished on lawns, and in the West this figure is 60 percent. The agency also claims that 10 percent of the air pollution in the United States is generated by lawn and garden equipment, and that gasoline spills from refueling lawn mowers, edgers, and the like add up to some 17 million gallons a year—far more than the 10.8 million gallons of crude oil spilled into Alaska's Prince William Sound in 1989 by the *Exxon Valdez*! And lawn, the quintessential monoculture of residential landscapes, offers little in the way of food and shelter for pollinators, birds, and other wildlife.

Living Without Lawn

Lawns are often considered essential outdoor living space, but decks and patios are good alternatives and have the additional advantage of requiring little or no maintenance. Most people also appreciate the fact that turf provides some open space around their homes. But there are scores of beautiful groundcovers that can play this role with a far smaller environmental footprint than turf. When homeowners think of groundcovers, three familiar standbys invariably come to mind: vinca (*Vinca minor*), pachysandra (*Pachysandra terminalis*), and English ivy (*Hedera helix*). However, vinca and English ivy are invasive species that rapidly invade forests in the East and Northwest. So it's a good idea to avoid them and instead do native pollinators and other wildlife a favor and look for the native

A carbon-neutral California garden designed by Douglas Kent features low-growing and mostly native flowers that provide more color and seasonal interest than conventional lawn.

VERTICAL LAYERS OF A FOREST

To capture and store the most carbon in your garden, pack in as many perennial and woody plants as possible. Mimic the way plants occupy every available niche in a forest, for example, by occupying various vertical layers. Below the forest canopy, formed by the tallest trees, are several other distinct vegetation strata: an understory of smaller trees; a shrub layer that consists of both shrubs and young trees; and a ground layer of wildflowers, ferns, and mosses.

species with which they have coevolved. In the dappled shade beneath the coastal forest of oaks, sassafras, and wild cherry in my Shelter Island, New York, garden, for instance, I've replaced lawn with various dainty violets such as Labrador violet (*Viola labradorica*), with maroon foliage, and fragrant sweet violet (*V. odorata*), which grows out of carpets of moss.

A favorite combination of many eastern woodland gardeners is creeping phlox (*Phlox stolonifera*), and foam flower (*Tiarella cordifolia*). In spring, the dense, eight-inch-tall spikes of pale to deep purple flowers of the phlox mingle with the foam flower's small, creamy-white flowers on upright stems. There are lovely native groundcovers for every region and for sun or shade, such as Oregon wood sorrel (*Oxalis oregana*), with shamrock-like leaves and funnel-shaped white or rose-pink flowers in the Northwest; bunchberry dogwood (*Cornus canadensis*), the shrublet relative of flowering dogwood trees with similar tiny white flower clusters surrounded by four white bracts for cool northern climes; or trailing indigo bush (*Dalea greggii*), with feathery, silvery-green compound foliage that sets off clusters of tiny rosy-purple flowers in the desert Southwest.

Once you've created your patio or deck and planted some groundcovers in the immediate vicinity of your home, turn your attention to one of the most important guidelines for climate-friendly gardening and capture as much carbon as you can by packing in as many woody and herbaceous perennial plants as possible. Ecologists use the term "niche complementarity" to describe how plants arrange themselves in natural ecosystems to take advantage of every available resource. Take your cue from nature and put niche complementarity to work in your garden by re-creating the layers of plant growth found in local woodlands. The topmost layer is the canopy, formed by the tallest trees. Below the canopy there are as many as three more distinct layers of mostly shade-loving vegetation. Just below the canopy is the understory of smaller trees, such as flowering dogwoods. Below the understory is the shrub layer, which consists of shrubs and small trees. Ferns, wildflowers, mosses, and other plants compose the tapestry known as the ground layer. For more on sequestering carbon in your vegetation, see page 95. For details on using niche complementarity as a model to boost productivity in the vegetable garden, see page 74.

Alternative Turfgrass Varieties

If you need a lawn, keep it small—a good rule of thumb is that if you can't mow it with a reel mower, it's too large. And consider using a turfgrass variety that requires little or no mowing and irrigation.

During the past couple of decades, a number of low- and no-mow grasses have been developed for various climate regions. A smaller climate footprint isn't their only virtue—unlike conventional lawns, these new grasses don't require constant watering, feeding, mowing, and weeding (or worse, herbicides), so instead of work-

Many people appreciate the open space around their home that lawn provides. Lovely ground-covers like bunchberry dogwood can do the same without turf's huge climate footprint.

ing, you can spend time watching butterflies flit among your flowers, or doing whatever it is you love to do.

In California, irrigation and horticultural professionals have launched the Grass Roots Program, an effort to wean residents of the Golden State from water-guzzling Bermuda grass and fescues, which originate in wetter climates but make up 99 percent of California lawns. These traditional turfgrasses soak up 40 to 50 percent of the state's potable water, already in short supply, and 7 percent of its energy is consumed to transport this water to consumers. As an alternative, the Grass Roots Program is promoting UC VERDE (*Buchloe dactyloides*) a buffalograss cultivar developed in California for the state's climates that rates twice as high as other turfgrasses for drought tolerance and reduced water use, pest and disease resistance, and density. In fact, UC VERDE requires 80 percent less water than tall fescue and 40 percent less water than Bermuda grass—no small consideration in an arid state that has been suffering a decade-long drought. What's more, it grows slowly, to four to six inches tall, and no set cutting schedule is necessary. Even for neatnicks addicted to the manicured look, mowing once a month is sufficient.

A relative newcomer to home lawns, buffalograss is native to the Great Plains, from Minnesota to Montana and south into Mexico, growing wherever conditions aren't too moist, too sandy, or too shady. However, cultivars have now been developed that can be grown in suitable conditions in the eastern two-thirds of the United States. In very dry areas, the even more drought-tolerant blue grama

Some new turfgrass varieties require little or no mowing and irrigation. This blue grama lawn in New Mexico is very drought tolerant and needs only occasional mowing for a manicured look.

(*Bouteloua gracilis*) is sometimes used to ensure solid color throughout the dry season. In roughly the northern third of the country and in southern Canada, mixes of low-growing fine fescues are a good alternative. They require mowing only once or twice a year—if that—need little if any irrigation once established, and thrive in full sun to partial shade. Contact your county Cooperative Extension office for more information on which alternative turfgrass varieties are best suited to your area.

To minimize turf's climate footprint, leave the clippings on your lawn when it is time to mow. This not only minimizes the energy needed to transport the clippings to the local landfill, it also reduces the need for nitrogen fertilizers and their resulting emissions of nitrous oxide and other greenhouse gases.

Feed the Soil, not the Plants

For centuries, conventional horticulture has inadvertently amounted to a form of soil abuse. From the moment we begin gardening, we're taught the importance of turning over the soil. In his no-till manual *Weedless Gardening*, Lee Reich blames it all on Jethro Tull. The 18th-century farmer and writer, Reich says, "advocated thorough pulverization of the soil on the (wrong) assumption that plant roots could most efficiently gobble up the resulting small soil particles." Today, although we know that plants don't eat soil particles, we're told we need to constantly cultivate the soil to loosen it up and facilitate aeration.

Under the impression that twice as much aeration is twice as good, the most dedicated gardeners actually perform the masochistic if well-intentioned practice called double digging—digging out a trench, mixing organic matter in the bottom of the trench, then turning over adjacent soil into it, in effect creating another trench that can be filled with organic matter. And so on, until the entire garden has been upended. But one result of such backbreaking effort is that the shot of oxygen afforded by cultivation overstimulates soil microorganisms. They proceed to rapidly burn up the soil's organic matter—its storehouse of carbon—which literally disappears into thin air in the form of carbon dioxide. In addition to CO_2, disturbed soils also release the powerful greenhouse gases methane and nitrous oxide.

Rototilling is a similarly destructive practice. It also destroys the soil structure created by the various members of the soil food web. In addition, it wrecks earthworm burrows and soil passages. In the process, it actually reduces the ability of the soil to hold water and air.

To make matters worse, we "feed" our plants with fertilizer. American gardeners have been led to believe that applying fertilizer to plants is as fundamental as brushing our teeth. "Most gardeners are surprised to learn that often the biggest contributor to greenhouse emissions from home gardening and lawn care is associated with use of nitrogen fertilizers," says David Wolfe, professor of plant and soil ecology at Cornell University. In terms of total greenhouse gas emissions, manures and other organic sources are better than synthetic fertilizers because the CO_2 emissions associated with manufacture are mostly eliminated. But using either synthetic or organic fertilizers releases nitrous oxide gas.

We ship garden "waste" off to the local landfill, which not only robs the soil of organic matter and nutrients, making applications of store-bought fertilizers and soil amendments necessary, but also results in increased emissions of methane. According to the EPA, decomposition of wastes in landfills is one of the two largest sources of methane emissions in the United States.

Actually, the soil abuse starts before our homes are even built, when the land is first being developed. The contractors arrive with their heavy machinery, bulldozing existing vegetation and compacting the soil. This depletes the soil's

Cultivation overstimulates soil organisms, depleting organic matter and releasing carbon dioxide, methane, and nitrous oxide.

THE COMPOSTING CONTROVERSY

Landscape designer Douglas Kent swears he almost had a fight over the relative merits of composting versus sending excess yard waste to a dump. "I got on my soap box at a garden center once and began explaining the benefits of tossing our green waste in a landfill to the manager and several customers," he writes in his book, *A New Era of Gardening*. Within minutes he was "verbally attacked" by a shopper who worked at the local recycling center, where they are extremely proud that they are helping to slash the amount of yard waste going to landfills by 50 percent.

Kent contends that a landscape can be a carbon sink only if some of its vegetation, in his words, "never ever decomposes." For this reason, he recommends composting only as much green waste as necessary to renew your soil. New gardens, says Kent, require a lot more compost than older, established gardens do. In the latter case, he advocates sending excess trimmings to a state-of-the-art landfill, which he says poses little environmental risk but will "mummify" the biomass, storing it for many years with little or no decomposition.

Kent is correct that composting is a source of greenhouse gas emissions. The same natural process of decomposition that happens every day in nature is also at work in a compost pile. Composting is essentially just decomposition speeded up. When we compost, we give fungi, bacteria, and other creatures everything they need to decompose leaves, grass clippings, and other garden trimmings quickly. As they decompose the organic matter, they also release some carbon dioxide into the atmosphere.

However, to calculate the greenhouse gas emissions that result from various waste options, including composting and landfills, the EPA follows internationally accepted guidelines that consider CO_2 emissions resulting from composting a natural part of the carbon cycle. According to this reasoning, the carbon in composted garden trimmings was originally removed from the atmosphere by photosynthesis and eventually would return to the atmosphere via decomposition. By contrast, the methane emissions that result from the anaerobic conditions in landfills would not be emitted if it were not for the human activity of landfilling the waste.

It's also important to note that landfills—including state-of-the-art facilities—are one of the largest sources of methane emissions in the United States. The EPA calculated that in 2004, landfills using advanced equipment to capture methane and other landfill gases were still responsible for 59 percent of all methane generated at landfills. Research suggests that properly managed compost piles do not generate methane emissions. In addition, once the compost is applied in the garden, some of its carbon is sequestered in the soil. For more on composting as a way to sequester carbon in garden soil, see page 80.

Regular applications of compost build up the level of organic matter in garden soil, enhancing fertility and sequestering carbon.

carbon and results in greenhouse emissions, degrades structure, and reduces its ability to absorb water, which increases storm-water runoff and soil erosion and the potential for flooding.

Protecting healthy soils and restoring degraded ones should be a high priority for developers and gardeners alike. Before any blueprints are drawn up, it's important to map out areas where the soil is healthy and where it has been disturbed by previous owners or users. Grading should be minimized, topsoil should be protected, and the soil should be disturbed as little as possible. That means protecting existing vegetation, especially trees.

And degraded soils should be made healthy again. For decades, while agriculture and horticulture were being revolutionized by fossil fuel–based fertilizers and pesticides, organic gardeners continued to emphasize the importance of organic matter to healthy soils. The father of the organic movement, Sir Albert Howard, a British government agronomist in India in the 1930s, began to suspect that the use of synthetic fertilizers was doing more harm than good—that it was like a shot of caffeine that produces a temporary spurt in yield. But they ultimately destroy the countless organisms, from microscopic fungi and bacteria to larger creatures such as earthworms and millipedes, that are the key to long-term soil fertility. To help maintain soil organic matter, Howard developed the Indore method of composting. His ideas are the foundation of the organic gardening adage "feed the soil, not the plant"—that is, maintain soil fertility by increasing its organic-matter

No-till gardening preserves the soil's organic matter. The mulch of compost and other organic materials applied to the top of the soil is a relatively rich and well-balanced food for plants.

content rather than applying the quick, and ultimately counterproductive, fix of synthetic fertilizers.

More recently, an increasing number of organic gardeners are adopting the no-till approach. The greatest benefit of no-till gardening—other than fewer weeds and an end to backbreaking cultivation, of course—is that the soil's organic matter, its carbon, is preserved. The mulch of compost and other organic materials added to the top of the soil is a relatively rich and well-balanced plant food. In fact, together organic and no-till gardening eliminate the necessity of automatically sprinkling bags of fertilizer on garden plants. For more on no-till and other steps you can take to sequester carbon in your soil, see page 80.

Pass up Gourmet Potting Mixes

Not long ago, potting soil was something many people made themselves using a few simple ingredients. In recent years, however, this once-humble material has been transformed into an upmarket mixture of largely unnecessary components from around the globe. The amount of embodied energy and greenhouse gases associated with these high-priced designer mixtures is amazing.

It's virtually impossible these days to find a bag of potting soil that isn't loaded with synthetic fertilizer. Nitrogen fertilizer, as we've seen, is one of the typical gardener's biggest contributions to global warming.

The organic matter in the typical bag of potting mix could easily come from local sources, whether composted clamshells, composted pine bark, or composted garden trimmings. Instead, it's often shipped from far away. Those bags of potting media piled up at the local garden center are likely to contain Canadian peat moss and perlite transported from the Greek island of Milos. Peat moss—the partially decomposed remains of sphagnum moss from bogs, which are critical carbon sinks (see page 88)—traditionally has been used in potting soil because it has the ability to retain water and still allow oxygen to get to plant roots. An enormous amount of energy is required to produce perlite, because the raw product, a type of volcanic glass, needs to be heated to 1,600°F to become the lightweight white pellets found in most potting mixes. The resulting concoctions, which a South Carolina–based producer calls "potting soil on steroids," are packaged in plastic bags, then stacked and shrink-wrapped on wooden pallets for shipping to nurseries and superstores.

One alternative to these products is to make your own, using compost but not peat or perlite. A classic recipe for sustainable potting soil calls for one-third mature compost that has been screened, one-third garden topsoil, and one-third sharp sand. Other recipes are available online.

Fortunately for gardeners who want the convenience of prebagged potting mix, new products with a smaller climate footprint are becoming available. One of the first companies to produce these alternative mixes is Organic Mechanics Potting Soil. "Maintaining a low carbon footprint is a major part of our mission," says the company's president, Mark Highland. It buys most of its ingredients locally, such as compost produced in its home county in Pennsylvania, to help reduce the fuel consumption

The typical bag of potting soil has a huge climate footprint. The most sustainable mixes contain compost and coir, above, instead of peat moss, perlite, and synthetic fertilizer.

and CO_2 emissions involved with transporting materials. Other ingredients include pine bark, worm castings, and rice hulls.

Organic Mechanics uses coconut coir as an alternative to Canadian peat moss in some potting mixes. Coir, a renewable material from Sri Lanka, is dried and compressed, then transported by large container ships (reducing the climate footprint from transportation). Coir has the additional advantage of breaking down more slowly than peat, so the product lasts longer. The Organic Mechanics warehouse is heated with recycled waste oil and its equipment runs on biodiesel. The company even makes a point of distributing its mixes mainly within its region, from Long Island, New York, south to Washington, D.C., and west to Columbus, Ohio.

If alternative potting mixes are not available in your area, you can reduce your climate footprint by looking on the bag label to make sure that the potting soil you want to purchase includes no fertilizer but does contain compost, ideally compost made locally. Compost not only is nutrient rich, reducing the need for additional fertilizer, but also retains water better than peat. Keep in mind, though, that plants growing in containers generally require more water than those growing in the ground. Choose plants and containers accordingly. Soil in unglazed terra-cotta pots dries out quickly, for example, so avoid them unless you happen to be growing cacti and other succulents.

Strive for a No-Irrigation Garden

It's time to come to terms with the fact that water is becoming scarcer in most regions as climate change intensifies, and is too precious to lavish unnecessarily

With climate change already stressing water resources, it's more important than ever to create gardens, like this prairie planting, that require no irrigation once established.

on ornamental landscapes. This alone is reason enough to adapt gardens to the amount of precipitation that falls naturally in the area. The amount of embodied energy and resulting greenhouse gas emissions involved in pumping and distributing the water we use every day makes the case all the more persuasive. According to the EPA, American public water supply and treatment facilities consume about 56 billion kilowatt-hours annually—enough electricity to power more than five million homes for an entire year!

For the past decade or two, horticulturists have been singing the praises of xeriscaping, a system of low-water landscaping based on six practices, including limiting lawn areas; improving the water-holding capacity of soils by adding compost and other organic materials; using

A hand-painted rain barrel collects water elegantly and inexpensively for use in the garden.

water-conserving mulches; growing water-efficient plants suited to your climate; and irrigating efficiently and sparingly. So far so good. The final instruction, however, is to group plants with similar water requirements. This assumes that some of the plants require more irrigation than others—in other words, they're *not* all suited to the climate. That's no longer good enough.

To minimize your carbon footprint, select plants for the ornamental landscape that not only fit the amount of sun and type of soil in your yard but need no supplemental water in your part of the country once they're established—preferably, species that are native to your region and provide food and nesting places for birds and other wildlife, which are having their own problems coping with climate change.

Sometimes supplemental water is essential. Many plants, especially those with large leaves, which lose water more rapidly than small ones through transpiration, go through an acclimation period after being planted, commonly known as transplant shock. This is most common during summer months. In part it is due to all the agitation of roots that is typical during transplanting. New transplants need to be watched carefully throughout the first year, and watered when the soil dries out

Whether straw, pine needles, shredded leaves, bark chips, or compost, organic mulches not only enrich the soil and increase its carbon content but also conserve precious moisture.

or the plant looks stressed. What's more, vegetables can require one to two inches of water a week, depending on root depth, their stage of growth, and the type of soil you have.

How to Water Wisely

Here's how to conserve water in the garden and irrigate most efficiently in the few instances when it is truly necessary.

Apply mulch. Mulches such as shredded leaves, bark chips, pine needles, nutshells, or whatever organic materials are readily available, conserve precious soil moisture that otherwise would evaporate into the atmosphere. Mulch also has an array of other advantages. For more on mulching, see page 90.

Capture precipitation in rain barrels or cisterns to use for irrigation. The Sustainable Sites initiative, the new rating system for ecologically, economically, and socially beneficial landscapes, awards two points for gardens that reduce the use of potable water (whether from groundwater or rivers or other surface waters) by 75 percent from a baseline case. Three points are awarded for gardens that use no potable water for irrigation once plants are established; a garden that consumes no potable water both during and after establishment is awarded five points.

Using rain barrels to capture water flowing from your gutters is an inexpensive way to avoid employing potable water for necessary irrigation. Rain barrels typically hold 54 gallons and come with a screened cover and outlet hose. Of late, designers have been creating stylish variations on the humble rain barrel and expensive cisterns. The Rainwater HOG, for example, is a system of 47-gallon plastic tanks with a sleek profile that can fit along narrow passages, under decks, or in other underused spaces. The modular design enables you to add on capacity and even put the tanks in multiple locations. If you prefer a funkier look, the Rainpod looks like a miniature municipal water tank topped with a Statue of Liberty–like crown that captures the precipitation. Propped up on three legs made of local timber and looking like a little UFO that's landed in your yard, it stands a bit taller than the average person so the water can be delivered gratis by gravity.

A cistern, typically a tank that stores rainwater underground, is a more complicated undertaking but can store a lot more water than a rain barrel. Check with your local Cooperative Extension office for information on the best systems for your region and how to construct them.

Use a rain gauge to measure weekly rainfall. If there hasn't been enough rain to sustain your plants, apply only the amount of supplemental water needed, no more.

Avoid frequent watering. One thorough watering each week is best; irrigating more often encourages shallow roots and can weaken plants. To reduce water loss via evaporation, don't water during hot, windy parts of the day. Early-morning watering is preferable because wetting foliage in the evening can increase your plants' susceptibility to diseases.

Hand watering and low-pressure, low-volume systems such as drip irrigation are the most efficient ways to supplement natural precipitation when necessary.

Plants in plastic containers and other garden products can have substantial climate footprints. Look for items that have been certified "green" by an independent organization.

Hand water or use water-conserving low-pressure, low-volume systems instead of traditional sprinklers. Drip irrigation devices apply the water right where your plants need it—at or near the root zone. They also reduce water loss due to evaporation, and the low flow rate minimizes the potential for water leaching below the root zone or running off the surface.

Purchase Certified Plants and Other Products

Garden products and services can be associated with substantial climate footprints, so it's worth seeking out manufacturers who make the effort to slash their greenhouse gas emissions. With just about every company rushing to polish its environmental credentials these days, it's getting downright difficult to distinguish the truly green from the greenwashed. Look for products and services that have been certified by an independent organization that has determined they meet a set of environmentally rigorous standards. The group behind an eco-label should make information on its organizational leadership and funding, as well as the standards it uses to certify products, available to the public. Following are a few that are particularly useful for gardeners.

When you're shopping for container plants and even cut flowers, look for the Veriflora label. Veriflora evaluates growers, distributors, wholesalers, and florists according to stringent sustainability standards that cover the entire life cycle of these products, from soil preparation and seed planting through production, harvest, post-harvest handling, and distribution for sale. For example, companies that wish to be certified need to demonstrate they have adopted practices that build and maintain healthy soil structure and functioning. They are required to seek the most energy-efficient methods for growing, transporting, and handling crops by supporting local and regional production and distribution and minimizing the use of fossil fuels.

In addition, Veriflora addresses climate change head on by providing a method to account for greenhouse gas emissions and sets goals for reducing them. To meet the goals built into the Veriflora standards, companies must submit plans detailing how they will, among other things, reduce net greenhouse gas emissions up to 30 percent by 2025, and increase total carbon sequestration in their soils by 25 percent over the next 25 years. The goals could be more aggressive, but they're a start. You can find a list of certified companies and products on the Veriflora website.

The Organic Materials Review Institute, or OMRI, is an independent reviewer of products used by certified organic growers and suppliers. Organic products typically are not as energy intensive to produce as petrochemical products, and because they're not synthesized from fossil fuels, they're likely to have a smaller climate footprint.

The OMRI Products List, a directory of all products the organization has determined are allowed for use in organic production, processing, and handling, includes everything from earthworm castings to composts and mulches. Available on the organization's website, the easy-to-use database can be searched by product (compost tea, say, or potting media), category (such as soil amendments), or manufacturer. Contact information for each manufacturer is provided, making it relatively easy to track down a particular product.

If you're in the market for a water-conserving irrigation system, it's worth checking out WaterSense. Sponsored by the EPA, WaterSense seeks to do for irrigation products and services and plumbing fixtures what the Energy Star label has done for electric appliances. Irrigation technologies and services that have been awarded the WaterSense label are listed on the program's website.

Use Materials with a Small Climate Footprint

Whether wood, recycled plastic lumber, or brick, the materials used to manufacture decks or fences, pave paths and patios, or create containers, chairs, and other outdoor furniture vary widely in climate impact. Following is a guide to choosing materials that minimize your landscape's climate footprint.

A GUIDE TO LANDSCAPE MATERIALS AND PRODUCTS

KELLY OGRODNIK

Choosing sustainable landscape materials is no easy task—one day we hear that recycled plastic lumber is better than concrete, and the next day we're told that locally harvested wood is better than recycled plastic lumber. As sustainability becomes a priority, solid data on the environmental impacts of wood, stone, and other materials is emerging. This offers designers and consumers the ability to make better-informed decisions about the types of products to use in their landscapes.

Measuring Impacts

"Researchers across the globe are still struggling to come to a consensus on the issues involved in carbon footprint analysis," says Melissa Bilec, assistant director of the Mascaro Center for Sustainable Innovation at the University of Pittsburgh. A carbon-impact analysis can include a wide variety of parameters, including how the material is extracted or harvested; the distance it travels from where it is harvested or extracted to a manufacturing plant; the energy consumed and pollutants emitted during the manufacturing process and the energy necessary to transport it from the factory to the store and ultimately to your garden; the resources required to install it; and the environmental impacts associated with its disposal. Some assessments are more complex than others; not all take into consideration each and every parameter.

Online carbon footprint calculators vary dramatically in depth of analysis and do not always tell the whole story. For example, some calculators limit their analysis from extraction to consumption, while others take it one step further by including disposal. A more in-depth and highly refined tool known as life cycle assessment takes into consideration a range of impacts and end-of-life scenarios, such as recycling or landfilling, to more fully determine the environmental footprint of a product.

Reusing existing and salvaged materials, such as the brick used to pave this patio, is better than buying new.

One of the most popular landscape materials, concrete is very energy intensive to produce. Recycled concrete or products containing a cement substitute are good alternatives.

Because there are still so many uncertainties involved in embodied carbon analysis, it's a good idea to defer to the basic principles called the 3 Rs—reduce, reuse, and recycle—to help minimize your impact on the environment when purchasing landscape materials and products.

Reduce. First, ask yourself if you absolutely need to have that new patio or fence. If you decide to move forward with new construction, a good rule of thumb is to choose products that are local, made of natural materials, sustainably harvested, and untreated. Fossil fuels burned to transport materials can have a significant impact on a product's carbon footprint, so look for materials that are harvested or extracted, manufactured, and sold locally. Do you know of a local carpenter who can purchase locally harvested wood and build your fence on-site? If you are creating a patio or path, is there a nearby supply store that carries locally mined stone, or a local manufacturing plant that fabricates pavers from materials obtained in your region?

Reuse. Reusing existing and salvaged materials is not only more environmentally friendly than purchasing materials made from virgin resources, but it also is often less expensive. Do you or a neighbor have a stockpile of bricks behind the garage that could be used for a new patio, or stones that could be employed to create a new path? Can the wood from your current deck be incorporated in a new design? Remember the phrase "one person's trash is another person's treasure"? Stores that sell reusable building materials are becoming more prevalent, and web-based groups such as Salvaged Building Materials Exchange, Craigslist, and Freecycle offer less-expensive (or free!) options for secondhand and like-new materials.

Recycle. Products made partially or entirely from recycled material are becoming widely available, whether because it is cheaper for the manufacturer or because of the minimized environmental impact. Reducing the demand for virgin material slows the rate of depletion of valuable natural resources. It also minimizes the consumption of energy that otherwise would be necessary for creating new products, as well as the energy and land necessary to transport wastes and dispose of them in a landfill. An increasing variety of products with recycled content are available, such as recycled plastic lumber, mulch made from recycled rubber tires, and concrete containing reclaimed fly ash from coal combustion.

What to Choose?

When faced with a range of options for landscape materials—one made from virgin materials, one with recycled content, another made from local materials—how do you determine which product is best? Without an in-depth carbon footprint analysis or life cycle assessment, the comparison can be tricky. As research evolves, the complexities surrounding the environmental impacts of materials and products are sure to diminish. Until we have all the answers, it's useful to evaluate products and materials based primarily on the environmental impacts of the processes used to manufacture them, on which there is a good deal of existing data.

Wood Of all common building materials, wood requires the least amount of energy consumption and releases the smallest amount of CO_2 during processing. Throughout their lifetime, trees capture and store CO_2 and have the ability to retain the majority of it for many years, even after being harvested and milled. Trees are renewable, and wood is often reusable. However, keep in mind that wood may require maintenance

Wood has the smallest climate footprint of all common building materials. Local salvaged wood is the best choice, followed by wood certified by the Forest Stewardship Council.

throughout its lifetime, and it is important to choose the least toxic protective coatings. And even with regular maintenance, wood may not last as long as a manufactured substitute.

When choosing wood for a deck, fence, walkway, or patio furniture, look for a supplier that carries lumber that has been locally harvested or salvaged from discarded trees. Wood that has been certified by the Forest Stewardship Council (FSC) or Sustainable Forestry Initiative (SFI) is another good option, but be sure to choose material that has been harvested locally rather than shipped across the continent or from the tropics. To eliminate the off-gassing or leaching of toxins into the air, soil, and water, do not purchase wood that has been treated with chemicals.

Recycled Plastic Lumber and PVC Recycled plastic lumber is gaining popularity as a landscape material because it requires less maintenance than wood. It is usually made from recycled high-density polyethylene or recycled polyvinyl chloride (PVC). Recycled plastic lumber decks, fences, and play equipment are durable, competitively priced, and available in a variety of colors.

The environmental advantage of such products is their recycled content. One disadvantage is that more energy is required to produce recycled plastic material than to process wood. If the material contains PVC, the environmental impact jumps dramatically, as PVC is one of the most environmentally damaging of all plastics due to the release of greenhouse gases and toxic pollutants like dioxins during production. What's more, the manufacturing of recycled plastic products still requires a small percentage of virgin plastic.

Concrete, Cement, and Stone While concrete is one of the most commonly used construction materials in the world, with a variety of landscape uses, it is also one of the most energy intensive to produce. Concrete is made from a mixture of cement, aggregate, water, and various chemicals. The main ingredient in concrete is cement. When it is manufactured, cement must be heated in a kiln at about 2,700°F, consuming a massive amount of energy and emitting enormous amounts of carbon dioxide.

If your project requires concrete, look for a product that contains a cement substitute like recycled fly ash or slag that does not require the same energy-intensive manufacturing process. Recycled concrete is an additional paving option for a driveway, pathway, or patio. Taking advantage of existing materials minimizes manufacturing energy requirements and eliminates the need for disposal. Recycling concrete is a relatively simple process: Existing concrete is broken, removed, crushed, and screened. It can then be used as crushed gravel for a pathway or patio or as an aggregate base for a driveway, reprocessed as poured concrete for a patio or other hardscape feature, or made into concrete pavers.

Crushed limestone, crushed granite, and other aggregate alternatives are also valuable substitutes for concrete or cement. The processing of crushed materials is much less energy intensive since it does not require binding or a high-heat manufacturing process.

Offsetting Carbon Emissions in Your Garden

Janet Marinelli

You've probably heard the term "carbon offset." Carbon offsets have become the hottest green consumer products since reusable grocery bags. In the best of all possible worlds, taking steps to reduce your greenhouse gas emissions, whether in the house, in the garden, at work, or in transit, would get you to carbon neutral, with no net contribution to global warming. But even with your best efforts, it's almost impossible to shrink your climate footprint to zero.

One way to address your remaining climate impact is to pay for an equivalent amount of greenhouse gas reductions to be made somewhere else. This is known as carbon offsetting, and it involves investing in projects like wind farms and tree planting. The reductions from these projects are sold as carbon offsets by a growing number of vendors around the globe. On their websites, there is generally a carbon calculator that determines the greenhouse emissions resulting from, say, a flight from New York to Los Angeles, along with set fees per ton to offset or compensate for the carbon. For carbon offsetting to be effective, the vendor must invest the revenue generated from your purchase in projects that demonstrably reduce emissions of climate-altering gases.

Problem is, it can be difficult for purchasers to figure out which offsets deliver the biggest benefit, and which vendors they should buy from. To make things even more complicated, neither the vendors nor the offsets they sell are regulated, leading some observers to compare the offset market to the Wild West. Others have compared the offsets themselves to the medieval indulgences put up for sale to raise money for the church or enrich unscrupulous clerics. Catastrophic climate change will only be averted if individuals and organizations make substantial cuts in greenhouse gas emissions through their own activities. Carbon offsets are a useful supplement to these actions, but they shouldn't replace them.

Because no one has yet devised a carbon calculator for both building and maintaining a garden (see page 32), there's no easy way to determine your landscape's climate footprint or to precisely quantify the reductions achieved by reducing your use of water, fertilizer, or power tools so you can purchase offsets for your remaining emissions. However, there are steps you can take in your own yard to "offset" your overall carbon emissions—designing a landscape that reduces the amount of energy required to heat and cool your home, for example, or growing food to avoid the carbon emissions associated with purchasing fruits and vegetables at supermarkets.

Carbon offsetting can involve investing in projects like wind farms to compensate for greenhouse gas emissions. You can also take steps in the garden to offset your overall emissions.

All landscape-related offsets are not created equal, however. Like other offsets, they should be assessed according to how well they meet recognized criteria. One of the most important criteria is "permanence." An offset needs to not only lead to a reduction in greenhouse gas emissions but also be irreversible. Because they result in a permanent climate benefit, energy efficiency and renewable energy projects are considered the highest-quality offsets. For instance, the turbines at a wind farm reduce fossil fuel consumption and greenhouse gas emissions. Even if one or more of the turbines were to stop working, the greenhouse gas reductions already made would not be canceled out.

Similarly, landscaping that increases home energy efficiency results in a reduction in energy consumption and greenhouse gas emissions. Even if the next owner were to come in and relandscape so that no further reductions were achieved, those that had already been made by conserving energy would not be affected.

On the other hand, offsets that rely on storing carbon, like planting trees or increasing the soil's organic matter content, are not considered permanent. If the trees were to be killed by fire or disease or the soil disturbed, much of their stored carbon would be released back into the atmosphere. That doesn't mean planting trees and amending your soil with compost are not worth doing, however, because both have many other benefits as well.

Tree planting has many benefits but is not a permanent carbon offset, because if the trees were to be killed by fire or pests, much of their stored carbon would end up back in the atmosphere.

Using plants to cast shade and block cold winds can reduce the climate impact of houses, which are responsible for 16 percent of the United States' greenhouse gas emissions.

Landscaping for Home Energy Efficiency

In the United States, heating, cooling, and lighting buildings consumes a great deal of energy. According to the federal Department of Energy and the EPA, 16 percent of U.S. carbon dioxide emissions are generated from the energy used in our houses alone; for all buildings, not just residences, the number is 40 percent. By designing a landscape that reduces the amount of fossil fuels needed to heat and cool your home, you can offset a lot of carbon.

An energy-conserving landscape utilizes trees, shrubs, groundcovers, and vines to provide cooling summer shade as well as insulation against heat loss in winter. It can funnel cool breezes into your indoor and outdoor living spaces during the dog days of summer and deflect winter's heat-robbing winds. It can perform aesthetic functions, too. A windbreak, for example, can define the space in your yard or patio and provide privacy while blocking blustery winds. And by using plants as a living air conditioner or an insulting blanket, you can soften your house's architectural edges with foliage and flowers while improving its performance.

What's more, an energy-conserving landscape can slash your utility bills. Strategic planting of trees and shrubs can save you up to 40 percent on your energy bill, according to the EPA.

Climatic Regions

Which energy-conserving landscape strategies make most sense depends on where you live. Through the years, various climate classification systems have been developed. For the purposes of energy-conserving landscaping, a simple scheme that divides the United States into four climatic regions—cool, temperate, hot and arid, and hot and humid—is sufficient. The cool zone includes the northern Plains and Midwestern states and northern New England. The temperate zone is a wide swath extending from the Pacific Northwest across the continent to southern New England and the mid-Atlantic states. The hot and arid zone more or less conforms to what is popularly known as the desert Southwest, including southern California, and the hot and humid zone runs from south-central Texas east to Virginia and Florida.

The Department of Energy recommends the following landscaping strategies for each region, listed in order of importance:

Cool
- Use windbreaks to protect your house from cold winter winds.
- Do not block the sun from reaching south-facing windows.
- If summer overheating is a problem, shade south and west windows and walls from the direct summer sun.

Temperate
- Make the most of the warming effects of winter sunshine.
- Make the most of cooling shade in summer.
- Deflect winter winds away from the house.
- Funnel summer breezes toward your home.

Hot and Arid
- Provide shade to cool roofs, walls, and windows.
- Landscape around your home so that it is cooled by evapotranspiration, the release of water vapor from the soil and plant surfaces into the atmosphere.
- Funnel summer breezes toward your home if it is cooled naturally.
- Deflect them away from your home if it is air-conditioned.

Hot and Humid
- Direct summer breezes toward your home.
- Make the most of summer shade with trees that still allow low-angle winter sunlight to warm your home.
- Avoid locating planting beds close to your house if they require frequent watering.

Planning the Landscape

To create the most energy-efficient landscape possible, it helps to start by drawing a plan. The more you familiarize yourself with your site's existing features, whether

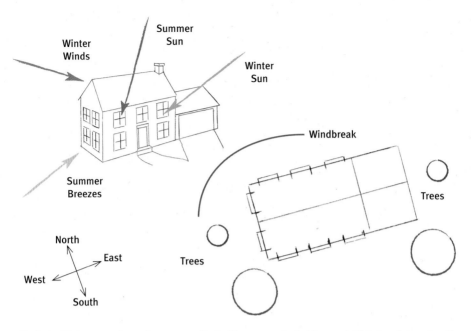

Noting which areas of your home are affected by sun and wind (upper left) helps determine the best placement of plantings to make it more energy efficient (lower right).

windows or pavement to be shaded or winds to be deflected, the better you'll be able to identify the most effective strategies.

Use paper and colored pencils to begin sketching your plan. Draw your house and property to scale, allowing about a quarter inch for each foot. Locate walks, driveways, and other paved surfaces, as well as the garage and other outbuildings. Mark all glassed areas, such as windows and doors—sunlight streaming through east- and west-facing windows can overheat a house in summer, while south-facing glass can help keep it warm in winter. Also note the presence of any solar collectors or photovoltaic arrays, which should never be shaded. Measure the height of your house, a crucial consideration for blocking winds and shading walls and the roof.

Identify north, south, east, and west. Draw arrows to show the angle of the sun in both winter and summer in your area. Note, for example, how the sun strikes your house between 9 a.m. and 3 p.m. in winter, since a south-facing window or collector receives most solar energy between these hours. Staff at your local library can help you determine solar angles, and there are also solar-position calculators online. To plan for appropriate shade, determine how the sun strikes the house in summer. Don't forget the late afternoon when the sun is lower in the sky and shines directly through windows at a time when the house has already become hot over the course of the day.

Next, note the direction of prevailing winds. Generally, for example, in the East the coldest winds come from the north and west, while in the West they come from

Deciduous trees that shade a roof from the afternoon sun in summer can reduce indoor temperatures by as much as 8°F to 10°F. Come winter, their bare branches allow the sun in.

the north and east, but check online or with the staff at your local library if you're not sure. If a windbreak is an appropriate solution, it will need to block the path of these prevailing winter winds. Also mark the direction of summer breezes.

Once you've completed this basic sketch of your house and its exposure to sun and wind, you're ready to consider how to use windbreaks, fences, shade trees, and other plantings to reduce your climate impact and save energy on heating and cooling. Circle the areas of your home that require shade or can benefit from breezes, and those that need protection from the wind, then identify the most effective strategies.

Creating Shade for Summer Cooling

Using landscape shade to cool your home in regions where summer overheating is a problem is the easiest way to reduce your house's climate footprint. Solar heat passing through your windows and being absorbed through your roof is the main reason air conditioning is necessary; shading these areas is the most cost-effective way to reduce this solar heat gain. A well-planned landscape reportedly can eventually reduce a formerly unshaded home's summer air-conditioning costs by 15 to 50 percent.

Shading Air Conditioners

An easy way to get quick results is to shade your air conditioner. According to the Department of Energy, shading the unit can increase its efficiency by as much as 10 percent. Just be sure that any shrubs or vines planted near the compressor do not obstruct the air flow or impede access for repairs.

Vines

Trees take a while to grow, but you can moderate hot sunshine quickly using vines that clamber up strategically placed trellises. A wooden lattice put up to support the vines will itself lend a measure of shade from the very start. Permanent structures such as trellises are most appropriate in hot climates where blocking solar heat gain in winter is not counterproductive. Where wetness and humidity are a problem, keep the trellis at least a foot away from the house to allow for air circulation; in these areas air should be allowed to flow around the home, keeping the structure and surrounding soil dry to prevent mildew and rot. Be sure the trellis isn't under your eaves—you want any hot air that builds up between the trellis and the siding to be able to vent out the top of the trellis. Arbors or pergolas can help shade windows too, and are a better choice in temperate regions if the lower winter sun can still penetrate the windows to warm your house.

Next, turn your attention to annual vines, which grow quickly and can cover a large area by mid- to late summer. You can make your shading device twice as functional by growing vines that provide not only shade but also fruits or vegetables. Edible vines such as scarlet runner beans (*Phaseolus coccineus*), winter squashes, and loofah squashes are vigorous and fast growing. Ornamental vines are also good candidates, especially if they offer food and shelter for wildlife. For

example, cypress vine (*Ipomoea quamoclit*) and scarlet creeper (*I. coccinea*) provide nectar for hummingbirds, while moonflower (*I. alba*) attracts moths.

At the same time, you can plant perennial vines, which may take two or more years to cover an arbor or trellis as tall as your home's walls. But if they will block the sun in winter (and cannot be cut back drastically at the end of the season), avoid planting these in cooler climates where solar heat gain is desirable during the cold months. Edible perennial vines for warm-winter areas include chayote (*Sechium edule*), kiwi (*Actinidia chinensis*), and passion flower

Placed strategically, vines like passion flower can shade walls and windows.

Shrubs and small trees such as redbud can play a role in an energy-conserving landscape by shading east- and west-facing windows from morning and afternoon sun.

(*Passiflora caerulea* and *P. edulis*). Native perennial vines with wildlife appeal include trumpet creeper (*Campsis radicans*), coral honeysuckle (*Lonicera sempervirens*), California honeysuckle (*L. hispidula*), and orange honeysuckle (*L. ciliosa*), which are all beloved by hummingbirds; wild grapes (*Vitis* species), which are eaten by many birds; and pipevines (*Aristolochia* species), which have interesting pipe-shaped flowers. Species such as Dutchman's pipe (*A. durior*) and California pipevine (*A. californica*) are host plants for the caterpillars of pipevine swallowtail butterflies.

Trees and Shrubs

Large trees and shrubs take longer to fill in but ultimately provide the best cooling shade. You've probably noticed how much cooler it is under a tree on a hot summer day than out in the sun. The air temperature under trees can be as much as 25°F cooler than that along nearby blacktop. As is true for vines, in cool and temperate climates placing trees for summer shade and winter sunshine is more complicated than it would first appear. What you want is a cooling device for summer that won't block out warming winter sunlight.

Trees can reduce summer temperatures significantly, especially when they're located on the south and west sides of the house. Large specimens that shade the roof from the afternoon sun can reduce indoor temperatures by as much as 8°F to 10°F. Make sure you choose trees tall enough when mature to shade your roof; if they don't overhang the roof, they won't cast much shade at midday when the sun is high in the sky. Set the trees close enough to the house to cast shade but far enough away, about 15 feet, that their roots won't damage your foundation. Also consider how wide the trees will become when mature and space them accordingly.

On small city or suburban lots, the optimum location for a shade tree may be in your neighbor's yard. Work with your neighbors to plan and plant an energy-conserving neighborhood landscape that improves conditions and lowers costs for everyone. If that's not possible, use shrubs and vines to shade your walls, windows, and air conditioner.

Deciduous trees provide shade in summer, then drop their leaves in autumn, allowing the warmth of the sun to filter through their bare branches and help heat the home when the weather is cold. Maples and other tall species with broad leaves and a high spreading crown are ideal for this purpose. As few as two or three properly spaced trees with wide crowns may suffice, depending on the size of your house. Limb them up, pruning lower branches for maximum heating of your walls and roof by the low winter sun.

A six- to eight-foot deciduous tree planted near your home will begin shading windows the first year. Depending on the tree species and the height of your home, it will shade the roof in five to ten years. Because some tall shade trees take a long time to top out, you may want to mix fast-growing trees among the more desirable slower-growing ones. As the slow growers mature, you can remove the fast-growing ones. Put them to good use in your garden or donate them to local woodworkers or artists to continue to sequester the carbon. For information on trees that capture the most carbon, see page 98.

Smaller trees and shrubs can play a role in an energy-conserving landscape as well. Species with branches lower to the ground can be planted closer to the house than tall shade trees and used for shading east- and west-facing walls and windows from the lower morning and afternoon sun. For the greatest ecological benefit, select species native to your region that offer food and shelter for pollinators and other wildlife, such as dogwoods (*Cornus* species) and redbuds (*Cercis* species). Shrubs planted close to the house will fill in rapidly and shade walls and windows relatively quickly. In wet and humid areas, avoid planting them right up against the house so air can circulate freely.

Espaliers are also good shading devices. They can be trained in a variety of interesting shapes. And because apples, pears, and other fruit trees are traditional candidates for espalier, they offer food as well as cooling shade.

Blocking the Wind for a Warmer House

Almost everyone has heard about the phenomenon of windchill in weather reports—if the outside temperature is 10°F, say, and the wind speed is 20 miles per hour, the windchill is −24°F. In other words, wind makes winter cold significantly worse. Although it's more difficult to use plantings to shape the wind than to shade the sun-

Winter winds

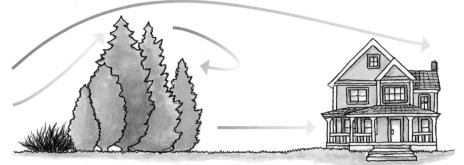

The most effective way to protect a home from winter cold is to plant a windbreak perpendicular to the prevailing winds. Two or three rows of evergreen trees are ideal. Some air will be able to pass through the windbreak, but most will be lofted up and over the house.

light, it is possible to keep a house warmer in winter by blocking the chilling effects of the wind. The most effective way is to plant a windbreak, a band of evergreen trees and shrubs located perpendicular to the prevailing winds. Hedges, wooden fences, and garden walls can also help obstruct and redirect the wind.

According to the Department of Energy, if you live in a windy area, strategically placed trees and shrubs can slash your winter heating bills by a third. And of course, when you reduce your consumption of fossil fuels, you not only cut your energy costs but also your greenhouse gas emissions. Windbreaks have other benefits as well. They can help block undesirable views and provide a living screen for privacy. Well-designed windbreaks are also aesthetically pleasing in themselves. And they're also great wildlife habitat. In fact, studies have demonstrated that the windbreaks in the Plains states, which were promoted in the mid-1930s to reduce soil erosion, are important stopover habitats for migrating birds.

When wind strikes an obstruction, it can move over, around, or through it. Therefore, to be most effective, a windbreak must meet certain requirements. The extent of protection is related to a windbreak's height and length. A windbreak will reduce wind speed for a distance of as much as 30 times its height. But for the greatest protection, plant your windbreak at a distance from your house of about two to five times the height of the trees when they're mature. That means that if the trees you're planting will grow to 40 feet tall, you should plant them at least 80 feet upwind from your house. A good windbreak provides protection in more than one direction. A study in South Dakota found that windbreaks located to the west, north, and east of homes cut their fuel consumption dramatically—by an average of 40 percent. Houses with windbreaks planted only on the windward side, the side of the prevailing winds, averaged 25 percent less fuel consumption than similar but unprotected homes.

Evergreen trees and shrubs are the most common kind of windbreak. The best windbreaks block the wind close to the ground as well as up high, so be sure to include species that have low crowns, such as spruces and firs. Evergreens can also be combined with a wall, fence, or earth berm to lift the winds up and over your house.

Some air should be able to pass through the windbreak, however. Impenetrable barriers create a strong vacuum on the protected or leeward side, causing some of the wind to whip up over the top and down, slamming into your house instead of lofting over it. Windbreaks composed of living plants naturally allow some of the wind to penetrate, which makes them more effective. If you're using a fence, use an open-weave pattern or remove every other slat.

The depth of the windbreak, not just its height and length, is important because it determines how much wind will be able to pass through. Three rows are ideal, but a two-row windbreak is still effective, and one row of evergreens is better than nothing if space is limited. How far apart the trees and shrubs should be planted depends upon the size and shape of the species when they reach maturity, but there should be no gaps between the plants when they are fully grown. If your budget allows, for quick cover, you can plant them at half the optimum spacing and remove every other one as they fill in. You can use them as Christmas trees, then for mulch when the holidays are over. If snow tends to drift in your area, plant low, multistemmed shrubs such as red-twig dogwood (*Cornus sericea*) on the windward side (outside) of your windbreak. Called a "snowtripper," this row of shrubs will reduce the amount of snow deposited near your house.

As with any type of landscaping, think diversity when selecting plants for your windbreak. Plant at least two to three different species and preferably more (see page 70). That way, if a pest or disease attacks, at least some of the trees will survive. One of the rows should include a dense evergreen species such as white

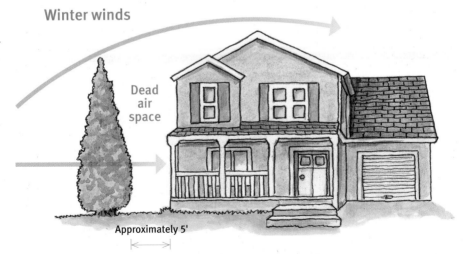

Winter winds

Dead air space

Approximately 5'

On small city or suburban lots, a dense evergreen hedge planted perpendicular to the prevailing wind several feet away from the house can help keep it warm in winter. This living wall creates a dead air space, which has much less chilling power than full-force wind.

or Colorado spruce or Douglas fir. White pine or other pines can be included in multirow windbreaks, but they're not as dense as spruces and tend to thin out even more as they mature. On small properties, red cedar and arborvitae are good choices. The leeward or inside rows can include smaller shrubs and flowering trees to add interest and increase the planting's value for wildlife. Native hollies (*Ilex* species), dogwoods (*Cornus* species), elderberries (*Sambucus* species), witch-hazels (*Hamamelis* species), and viburnums (*Viburnum* species) are all good wildlife plants and lovely additions to the landscape.

Not every property is big enough to accommodate a conventional windbreak. If you live on a small city or suburban lot, you can use less-substantial evergreen plantings closer to your house to help provide insulation. These can also be used along with windbreaks on large properties for additional protection. For this type of planting, dense evergreens that will grow into a thick hedge are most appropriate. Plant them close enough together to form a solid living wall and several feet away from your house to create a dead air space, which has much less chilling power than blustery wind. An evergreen planting can also help shelter a front or back door exposed to the wind.

SOME EVERGREENS FOR WINDBREAKS

Following are some evergreens native to the United States that are good candidates for large windbreaks and smaller plantings. Choose species suitable for your region and conditions.

Abies concolor, white fir

Abies fraseri, Fraser fir

Calocedrus decurrens, incense cedar

Chamaecyparis thyoides, Atlantic white cedar

Cupressus arizonica, Arizona cypress

Ilex opaca, American holly

Ilex vomitoria, yaupon

Juniperus scopulorum, Rocky Mountain juniper

Juniperus virginiana, eastern red cedar

Picea glauca, white spruce

Picea pungens, Colorado spruce

Thuja occidentalis, eastern arborvitae

Arborvitae is a good choice for creating a windbreak on small properties.

To direct summer breezes to a porch or patio or through open windows, plant rows of shrubs nearly parallel to the prevailing winds in a funnel shape that is widest away from the house.

Shaping the Wind for a Cooler Home

Finally, if you live in an area where prevailing summer and winter winds come from different directions, the same windbreak dynamics applied in reverse can be used to help cool your home and outdoor living spaces in summer. Instead of fending off the wind, these windbreaks and hedges funnel afternoon breezes toward the house or patio. Place them nearly parallel to the prevailing summer air currents, in a funnel shape that is wider away from the house and narrower closer up. This configuration can increase the breezes by up to 20 percent and can even be designed to force the air through your house's open windows.

It may seem beyond dispute that fruits and vegetables cultivated steps from the kitchen have the smallest climate footprint of any produce, but this depends on how they are grown.

The Climate Footprint of Homegrown Food
Amanda Knaul and Susan K. Pell

Local-food gurus have written a steady stream of books about the connection between large-scale food production and greenhouse gas emissions. In *The Omnivore's Dilemma*, author Michael Pollan challenges readers to think critically about the covert voyages of various foods from production to plate. Joan Dye Gussow describes the joys of growing produce in her New York garden in *This Organic Life: Confessions of a Suburban Homesteader*. Longing to support her family on fare enriched by fecund soils, novelist Barbara Kingsolver left the Arizona desert for more fertile Appalachia. *Animal, Vegetable, Miracle* chronicles the family's first year as "locavores" in Virginia.

Spurred by a 2003 Iowa University report that found most produce travels almost 1,500 miles before reaching the state's residents, the quest to assess the climate footprint of what we eat has focused on tallying "food miles," the distance food travels from field or pasture to table. However, the burning of fossil fuels during transport is far from the only source of greenhouse gas emissions associated with conventional food production. Other significant sources of greenhouse gases include the manufacture and transport of fossil fuel–derived fertilizers and pesticides, the heating and cooling of greenhouses, the use of petroleum-consuming farm equipment, and the refrigeration units and plastic packaging used for crop storage.

A crop's climate footprint depends not only on the practices of the farmer, but also on variables like the local climate and the specific requirements of individual crops themselves. Similarly, home or community gardeners may be more or less "carbon neutral," depending on their methods and materials.

Ecologists are teasing apart this complex relationship between food production and resource consumption. One interesting area of research, for example, focuses on the climate footprint of particular crops. University of Aberdeen researchers found that on farms in eastern Scotland, nitrogen-fixing leguminous crops such as beans and peas had smaller climate footprints than potatoes or winter cereals such as winter wheat. According to their study, which included data from conventional and organic as well as integrated farms (which combine both crop and livestock production in an interrelated system), organic farms had the smallest climate footprint.

Another study comparing the climate footprints of imported versus locally grown tomatoes and carrots in Sweden found that local is not always lower in embodied energy costs. Locally grown tomatoes had a larger climate footprint than those that were imported. In the case of the carrots, storage and transportation were the significant sources of greenhouse gas emissions, while for tomatoes, it was the fuel required for heating the greenhouses in which they are grown. In other words, choosing domestically or locally produced food over food that is imported may be a good general rule to follow, but strict adherence will not ensure that you are walking away with the smallest "feet."

Homegrown

It might seem beyond dispute that homegrown food, produced just steps from the kitchen, has the smallest footprint of all, but this is not necessarily the case. A study done by Garden Organic, the United Kingdom's leading organic growing charity, produced surprising results. The climate footprint of food grown by study participants was only slightly smaller than that of produce purchased from the grocery. Garden Organic attributes this to the fact that the gardeners were using more store-bought fertilizers and soil amendments than expected.

Home gardeners should not be discouraged by the complexity of climate footprint calculations, however. By growing your own food, you are certainly reducing the consumption of fossil fuels required to transport, store, and package food. But to maximize the climate benefits of homegrown food, you must also reduce greenhouse gas emissions further by minimizing the use of power equipment and store-bought fertilizers and other soil amendments, growing plants from seed instead of purchasing them in plastic containers and trays, building soil health, and conserving water. For details on how to reduce your garden's climate footprint, see page 31.

What's more, recent agricultural studies suggest a range of things you can do to sequester carbon in your garden, from increasing the level of organic matter in your soil to increasing your garden's biodiversity and productivity. For information on strategies to sequester carbon in your soil, see page 80.

Productivity and Permaculture

Like garden soil, garden vegetation can be a significant carbon sink. It has been estimated that annually, through the process of photosynthesis, 100 billion metric tons of atmospheric carbon are bound into carbon compounds. The more productive an ecosystem—that is, the more biomass it produces—the more carbon it can capture. Biologists conducting research on natural ecosystems have concluded that an ecosystem's productivity increases with its biodiversity. This may be partially due to what ecologists call "niche complementarity," a concept that describes the spatial relationships between plants and how they partition resources in the environment.

Gardeners are learning to put niche complementarity to work in the edible landscape. In a diverse garden, an array of plants with different cultural requirements will fill more niches and thus capture more carbon than the large monoculture farms that produce most of our food. Different plants have different characteristics and needs. Their roots reach to different depths. They take up water at differing rates. They absorb nutrients in disparate amounts; nitrogen-fixing legumes such as peas and beans can actually remove nitrogen from the atmosphere and add it to the soil. Different plants also take up carbon at different rates. For instance, woody plants tend to store a lot of carbon, so planting fruit trees and shrubs in a food garden can increase its ability to store carbon.

Achieving niche complementarity, and therefore increased productivity, is what permaculturists Bill Mollison and David Holmgren had in mind when they created a new model for home-scale gardens. Permaculture relies on a rule of thumb: *less input, more diversity.* Permaculture gardens are dominated by perennial plantings and "guilds," or associations of plants and animals, insects, fungi, and other organisms. Plants are chosen for their ability to create mutually beneficial relationships with other organisms. Perennials, rather than annuals such as radishes or tomatoes, are the plants of choice due to their lower fertilizer and maintenance requirements.

After realizing that his small perennial vegetable and herb beds were more productive and easier to manage than monocultures like his annual vegetable beds and orchard, British horticulturist Robert Hart pioneered forest gardening in the early 1960s. Based on his observation that woodlands, the most productive native ecosystems in the United Kingdom and other moist, temperate regions, are comprised of several distinct vertical layers, he transformed his small orchard into an "edible ecosystem" consisting of seven layers: the canopy of the original mature fruit trees, a low tree layer of smaller nut and fruit trees on dwarf rootstocks, a shrub layer of fruit bushes such as currants and berries, a herbaceous layer of perennial vegetables and herbs, a vertical layer of vines and climbers, a surface layer of cover crops, and a "rhizosphere" of root crops.

In *Edible Forest Gardens*, their two-volume manual for gardeners in North America's forested regions, Dave Jacke and Eric Toensmeier describe an edible forest garden as "a consciously designed community of mutually beneficial plants and animals" for the production of food as well as fuel, fiber, fodder, fertilizer, and "farmaceuticals." Forest gardeners need to become familiar with what Jacke and Toensmeier call the four aspects of forest ecology: architecture (the vertical layers), social structure (the food web, guilds, etc.), the underground economy (including soil fertility and structure and the soil food web), and succession (changes in the ecosystem over time).

Another basic way to promote diversity in your vegetable garden is to integrate traditional companion plantings. Companion plants form positive symbiotic associations by, for example, providing pest control or fixing nitrogen for their neighbors. The most familiar companion planting is probably the "three sisters" grown by Native Americans. It incorporates beans (which fix nitrogen in the soil), maize (which provides natural stakes up which the beans can grow), and squash (which covers the ground and suppresses weeds).

Companion plants can be low-carbon alternatives to many of the chemicals used to manage pests and weeds. Oregon State University researchers completed a study on beneficial insects and the plants that most appeal to them. Their findings were in line with other recent studies that conclude that members of the plant families Brassicaceae (mustard), Lamiaceae (mint), Apiaceae (carrot), and Asteraceae (daisy)

attract beneficial insects. Incorporating these plants in your garden can help keep pest populations in check. The roots and shoots of the Aztec marigold (*Tagetes erecta*) have been found to contain thiophenes and thiophene derivatives, chemicals believed to have nematicidal, insecticidal, and fungicidal properties.

"Nurse crops" act as physical barriers between valuable crops and insect pests and weeds. For instance, it has been observed that corn planted with squash disorients adult squash vine borers, while the squash's prickly vines help deter corn pests like raccoons. Tall sun

The marigolds interplanted with these cabbages discourage nemotodes and insects and suppress weeds.

lovers act as nurse crops for shorter, shade-loving plants, increasing their productivity. "Trap crops" act as lures for harmful insects. For example, interplantings of four-o'clocks (*Mirabilis* species) draw Japanese beetles away from food crops.

Seed Saving

Large-scale farms generally rely upon seeds mass-produced by big corporations. As a result, heirloom vegetable and fruit varieties that are adapted to the local climate are becoming rare. Heirloom varieties suited to the precipitation levels in your area will require less irrigation. By growing heirlooms selected for their proven disease resistance, you can also reduce your garden's dependence on pesticides. In addition, by saving and replanting your own seeds, you can avoid the greenhouse gas emissions associated with seeds that require long-distance transport and excessive packaging.

Just as important, growing heirloom varieties preserves the genetic diversity of crops. Monoculture farming has seriously compromised the genetic diversity of corn (*Zea mays*), for example, but home gardeners can help preserve disappearing heirloom varieties such as 'Strawberry', which is good for popping, and 'Blue Jade', a beautiful cultivar suitable for boiling. A range of heirloom potatoes (*Solanum tuberosum*), such as 'Purple Peruvian' and 'La Ratte', and garlics (*Allium sativum*), including 'Georgian Crystal' and 'Persian Star', help compensate for the lack of variety in these dietary staples at supermarkets. Eggplant (*Solanum melongena*) is another crop with an array of heirloom options, including the gorgeous 'Listada de Gandia'.

Nonprofit organizations like Seed Savers Exchange (SSE) and the Organic Seed Alliance support crop diversity and seed stewardship by offering membership discounts on heirloom seeds and provide tips for gardeners looking for creative ways to help build personal and community seed stocks, such as organizing seed swaps.

Like all science, research on the climate footprint of food is an ongoing investigation. Growing knowledge will continue to shape our crop choices and horticultural practices.

Growing plants from seed you collect yourself avoids the climate impact of transport and packaging.

LAYERS OF AN EDIBLE FOREST GARDEN

To achieve maximum diversity and productivity, permaculture gardens mimic the vertical layers found in surrounding natural areas. The edible forest garden below includes a canopy of shagbark hickory, a low tree layer of pear, and a shrub layer of blueberries and currants. Jerusalem artichokes are among the plants in the rhizosphere, and rhubarb grows in the herbaceous layer. The surface layer comprises strawberries, and a vertical layer of grapes ties the various vertical strata together.

Canopy

Low tree layer

Shrub layer

Vertical layer

Herbaceous layer

Rhizosphere

Surface layer

Turning Your Landscape into a Carbon Sink

Niall Dunne

As we've seen elsewhere in this volume, there are three key strategies for stabilizing and reducing the concentration of carbon dioxide and other greenhouse gases in the atmosphere: The first is to reduce emissions by becoming more energy efficient. The second is to develop clean-energy technologies, and the third is to capture carbon dioxide from pollution sources, as well as the atmosphere, and store, or sequester, it in natural and engineered sinks. The following chapter explores how homeowners can turn their gardens into natural carbon sinks.

Two types of carbon sequestration are possible: biotic and abiotic. Biotic sequestration harnesses the natural ability of plants to pull carbon dioxide from the air and store it in their tissues as cellulose and other organic compounds. It also involves soil organisms, which decompose dead plant matter and relocate some of the plant carbon underground as part of the organic component of the soil profile. Abiotic sequestration doesn't involve the use of living organisms. It's a high-tech solution that generally consists of collecting carbon dioxide emissions from power plants and other industrial sources, turning it into liquid form, and injecting it either deep into the ocean or deep underground in coal seams, old oil wells, and stable rock strata.

Abiotic sequestration technology is still mostly in the development phase and is largely untested. It will be very expensive and may take decades to become viable on a global scale. Biotic sequestration, in contrast, is a relatively straightforward and inexpensive proposition mainly involving the restoration of degraded natural areas, the cultivation of trees and other long-lived plants, and the sustainable management and conservation of soils. Biotic sequestration has limitations, as we'll see, but it is something that can be done, right now. What's more, it can be done on large and small scales.

The information that follows is about how home gardeners can get in on the action. It is divided into two sections, the first covering carbon sequestration in soil and the second covering sequestration in plants. Along with discussions of the biology behind carbon storage in plants and soils and an overview of the latest research on carbon sequestration, you'll find plenty of practical tips on how to make the most of your garden's natural ability to store carbon.

New studies on carbon storage in trees and other long-lived plants and in soils indicate which horticultural practices are good at preventing climate change and beneficial for the garden.

Typically, soils are only about one to ten percent organic matter, but globally more carbon is locked up in soil than in the atmosphere and living organisms combined.

Carbon Sequestration in Soil

Soil contains almost twice as much carbon as Earth's atmosphere and all its above-ground living organisms combined. About two-thirds of this soil carbon pool is bound up in organic matter, which includes the living fauna of the soil food web, decomposing plant and animal residues, and humus (the end product of decomposition). The rest is tied up in inorganic carbonate minerals such as calcite (calcium carbonate—the main ingredient in limestone), derived from the weathering of parent rock material, as well as from atmospheric sources.

Though the overall carbon pool is large, the percentage of carbon in most individual soils is relatively small. Soil organic matter—roughly half of which is carbon—makes up only about one to ten percent of most soils. (The variation is caused by differences in such factors as climate, vegetation type, and soil texture; generally, soil organic matter levels are higher in cooler, more humid regions, due to the combination of abundant plant life and low rates of decomposition.) But a little organic matter goes a long way when it comes to the health of your soil.

Plants pull carbon out of the air during photosynthesis and transform it into a variety of useful compounds (see "Carbon Sequestration in Plants," page 95). When plants die or shed their foliage in the fall, soil-based fungi and bacteria—assisted by an army of other organisms—get to work breaking down the carbon-rich plant tissues, liberating valuable nutrients into the soil in the process. Most soil fauna respire aerobically, so as they metabolize the plant residue, they absorb oxygen and release carbon dioxide. (Anaerobic soil organisms—primarily bacteria—also release carbon during respiration, in the form of methane, or CH_4, a powerful greenhouse gas.) Consequently, much of the carbon locked up in the plant material—up to 80 percent—is returned to the atmosphere relatively quickly. But a small portion of it is biochemically transformed by microbes into humus and becomes sequestered as part of soil's stable carbon pool.

In Praise of Humus

Humus is a spongy, dark-colored witches' brew of substances comprising about 60 to 80 percent of a soil's total organic matter. Much of it is very resistant to microbial decay: Some of the humic substances, as they are known, can last in undisturbed soils for hundreds or even thousands of years before eventually decomposing and releasing their carbon as CO_2. Mean residence time of humus in cultivated soils may be a lot lower—measured in years and decades rather than centuries.

Often referred to as "black gold," humus is the mainspring of a soil's natural fertility. Porous and cohesive, it builds and stabilizes soil structure, enhancing aeration and water-holding capacity. Studded with negative electrical charges, it's also very efficient at capturing mineral nutrients such as nitrogen, potassium, and calcium and making them available to plant roots. In addition, humus has the ability to buffer extremes of soil acidity and alkalinity, bind up harmful toxins, stimulate plant root growth, and suppress plant pathogens. (If you like the sound of what humus can do, then you'll be happy to know that adding compost to your garden soil will help increase its humus content; see "Compost: Making Your Own Humus," page 87.)

Historical Loss of Soil Carbon

The formation of humus by biological decomposition is the principal process by which carbon is sequestered in soils. But there are other processes too, such as aggregation, in which organic matter becomes bound together with clay and other soil particles into chunks, or aggregates (through a number of different forces, including the growth and extension of plant roots and fungal hyphae), and is physically shielded from microbial attack. Traditional farming practices—in particular, the use of the plow for tillage and seedbed preparation—disrupt these processes, eroding soil, harming beneficial soil organisms, and exposing stored carbon to the soil surface, where it is rapidly oxidized (combined with oxygen) by microbes and vented into the air as CO_2. With severe loss of soil carbon comes sharp declines in soil health and productivity.

It's estimated that conversion of natural ecosystems such as forests and grasslands to plow-based agriculture has depleted organic carbon in temperate climate soils by as much as 60 percent and in tropical soils by up to 75 percent. Much of the carbon was lost to the atmosphere, while the rest was washed away by erosion and redeposited in rivers and oceans. Restoring degraded soils by rebuilding their depleted organic carbon pools has enormous potential for offsetting carbon dioxide emissions. (It's worth noting that in arid regions, where soil organic carbon is naturally low, inorganic forms of carbon predominate and may also constitute an important sink for sequestration efforts. However, research on sequestering soil inorganic carbon is still in its infancy.)

Potential Gains and Limitations

Soil building is a very slow process, and it's unclear how much of the globe's historical soil carbon can be restored in a timely manner. However, many scientists are optimistic that soil carbon sequestration can play a major role in preventing or mitigating cataclysmic changes in the global climate. The Rodale Institute, a nonprofit research organization that promotes organic agriculture, reckons that globally, cultivated soils (if farmed organically) have the potential to offset nearly 40 percent of current carbon dioxide emissions. Rattan Lal, a professor in the School of Environment and Natural Resources at Ohio State University and the author of a number of influential research papers on biotic carbon sequestration, calculates more conservatively that soils have the potential to offset 5 to 15 percent of annual global fossil fuel emissions.

Rebuilding soil organic carbon stocks—and thus soil structure and fertility—is a win-win strategy: It not only offsets emissions but also generates a host of co-benefits, including increased biodiversity below- and above-ground, improved water quality, and healthier, more productive plants, which translates to more

Plow-based agriculture has depleted the organic carbon content of temperate-climate soils by as much as 60 percent. Much of the lost carbon was vented into the atmosphere.

Some 60 to 80 percent of the organic matter in soil consists of dark, spongy humus, much of which is quite resistant to releasing its stored carbon into the atmosphere.

carbon being sequestered in plant biomass, and in turn increased plant residues being added to the soil. This positive feedback loop eventually results in richer soil, increased humus formation, and more carbon entering the stable soil pool.

However, there are constraints. The natural capacity of soils to act as carbon sinks appears to be finite—that is, carbon added back into soil reaches a saturation point beyond which no more can be stored, regardless of further additions. Moreover, the sequestration is limited in duration: Because carbon eventually returns to the atmosphere through decomposition, the supply in the soil needs to be continuously replenished (whether through the restoration of natural carbon cycling processes or managed additions of plant residues), otherwise the sequestration process goes into reverse.

Increasing Carbon Levels in Farm Soils

So far, research on carbon sequestration in soil has been carried out almost exclusively in large-scale agricultural ecosystems, but the results of this research can also be used to develop guidelines for storing carbon in garden soils. To rebuild soil carbon pools on the farm, scientists recommend moving away from conventional cultivation practices, which rely on intensive tillage of the soil plus enormous inputs of synthetic fertilizer, and adopting more "restorative" techniques. The following techniques can be applied to smaller gardens as well:

• Regularly apply manures and other organic amendments.
• Reduce tillage.
• Convert to no-till gardening.

Red clover and other cover crops can help increase the carbon content of soil and prevent its loss through erosion.

- Plant cover crops to protect soil from erosion, add nitrogen, and increase organic matter.
- Use diverse crop rotations.
- Ensure an adequate supply of nutrients in the soil; humus formation is more efficient when adequate nitrogen, phosphorus, and sulfur are present—however, excess nitrogen fertilization stimulates the loss of carbon to the atmosphere and generates nitrous oxide emissions.
- Improve fertility to increase plant biomass and thus the amount of plant residue (for example, dead roots) that enters the soil carbon pool.
- Grow perennial crops, especially agroforestry crops wherever space permits.
- Allow surplus or marginal cultivated land to revert back to natural areas with native vegetation, which store more carbon because soil disturbance is lower and no carbon products are being harvested.

Several long-term experiments in Europe and the United States have demonstrated that organic farming methods result in higher rates of carbon sequestration than conventional farming with chemical fertilizers. For instance, a 27-year study conducted by the Rodale Institute showed that organic management of farm fields increased soil carbon levels by almost 30 percent, whereas conventionally managed plots showed no significant increase. No-till gardening (see page 91) has also been shown to increase soil carbon levels dramatically, at least in the upper layers of the soil profile, compared with conventional plow-based farming.

Another Reason to Go Organic

Although most gardens bear only a vague resemblance to farm fields, it seems pretty clear that adopting sustainable, organic techniques and minimizing soil disturbance is crucial to locking up carbon in garden soils and creating more climate-friendly gardens.

What kind of sequestration numbers are we talking about? As mentioned, the storage potential of soils varies with climate, type of vegetation, and soil texture. Gardeners in the Southwest may not have much luck with increasing soil organic carbon. The potential in the Northeast and other cool, humid climes is likely much greater.

To give one example: In 2000, Jon Foley, director of the Institute of the Environment at the University of Minnesota, carried out an informal study of his brother David's half-acre organic garden in Maine and came up with some impressive sequestration figures. Over a period of ten years, David had used compost mulches and cover crops to raise the level of soil organic matter (about 58 percent carbon) in the top eight inches of the garden's silt-loam soil from 1 percent to 7.7 percent. Jon calculated that this amounted to roughly 19 tons of carbon—about one year's worth of emissions produced by an average American!

Growing Soil Carbon in the Home Garden

Extrapolating from farm and forestry research, following are some basic guidelines for turning your garden soil into a carbon sink. The most important of them deal

The annual blanket of leaves shed by deciduous trees in autumn protects the soil and helps build carbon. Mulch serves the same function in gardens.

with minimizing disturbance of the soil and the regular application of organic mulches, such as compost.

Test your soil. Having your soil tested by a qualified laboratory is always a wise first step when beginning any new project in the garden. The lab analysis will tell you how much organic matter is in your soil and whether or not there are any nutrient deficiencies. The lab may also be able to tell you the natural or optimal levels of organic matter for the soil in your region, so you'll have a rough idea how much carbon your soil will hold.

Use organic amendments to address soil problems. If your soil suffers from nutrient deficiencies or other problems such as compaction or slow drainage, one option is to amend it with recycled organic conditioners like compost or composted manure before planting. These materials not only improve the physical environment of the soil and help build up soil carbon, they also provide a valuable source of slow-release nutrients for plants and food for humus-forming microbes. Organic conditioners are typically worked into soils at a rate of one inch for every six inches of soil. Before digging in any conditioner, make sure its carbon-to-nitrogen ratio is balanced at around 30:1. Amendments that are high in carbon, such as sawdust (200:1), can temporarily rob nitrogen from plants as they decompose and should be aged or composted before application (see "Compost: Making Your Own Humus," facing page). Applying organic amendments to the soil surface—mulching—can achieve the same curative results as incorporating them belowground, though over a much longer time period. Earthworms gradually pull the organic matter into the soil, improving soil structure and nutrient cycling.

Avoid fast-release nitrogen fertilizers (natural or synthetic). Excessive amounts of nitrogen in the soil can create nitrous oxide emissions and also have a negative effect on carbon sequestration. Using slow-release organic amendments and mulches should supply adequate nitrogen and other nutrients for most garden situations.

Soil tests can reveal how much organic matter is in your soil and whether nutrients are lacking.

COMPOST: MAKING YOUR OWN HUMUS

Compost is the dark, crumbly, sweet-smelling humus-like substance produced when organic materials are gathered into a pile and allowed to decompose. An inch-thick top-dressing of this "black gold" on your beds and borders every year is generally all you need to maintain a healthy soil and provide a balanced source of nutrients to your plants. And although 50 to 70 percent of the carbon in the raw materials of a pile are lost as CO_2 during decomposition, compost is nonetheless a rich source of relatively stable carbon, and using it is one of the easiest ways to sequester carbon in soil.

Unlike a neglected pile, a well-managed home compost pile produces little if any methane and nitrous oxide. Here are some tips on creating a perfect pile.

Carefully situate and enclose the pile. Locate your compost pile in a well-drained area of the garden that's shaded from the hot afternoon sun. Purchase or build a compost bin to protect the pile from marauding wildlife. A good-sized pile is about four feet in diameter and three feet high.

Add a mix of browns and greens. Compost microbes need a balanced diet of carbon (C) and nitrogen (N). Provide this by filling your bin with a mix of high-carbon "brown" materials, such as leaves, newspaper, and woody residues, and high-nitrogen "green" materials, such as grass clippings, kitchen scraps, and fresh cuttings from the garden. Finished compost has a carbon to nitrogen ratio (C:N) of about 30 to 1 by weight. If you start with too much brown material, the compost microbes will burn off a lot of the carbon as CO_2 to bring the ratio down. If you add too much green material, the microbes will adjust the ratio upward, and a lot of valuable nitrogen will be lost as ammonia gas. Give your microbes a C:N of 30:1 from the get-go—that is, a roughly even mix of browns and greens—and you'll conserve more carbon and nitrogen.

Provide air and moisture. The microbes that perform aerobic decomposition require a balance of air and water. Routine turning of your pile with a garden fork is recommended. However, too much air will dry out a pile and slow decomposition. A compost pile should feel damp to the touch, like a wrung-out sponge. If it's wet, turn your pile to increase aeration. If it feels dry, periodically add water as you turn over the compost.

Minimize emissions. Wet, low-oxygen conditions in a pile favor anaerobic microbes that release the powerful greenhouse gases methane and nitrous oxide. Turning your pile will help minimize these emissions, as will the following:

- Avoid layering brown and green materials on top of one another—this can create zones of anaerobic activity in the green layers. Mix them together instead.

- Limit the height of your pile to three feet, so the weight of the materials doesn't compress the air out of the bottom of the pile.

- Maximize airflow by shredding materials before adding them to the pile and building your pile on a foundation of coarse organic material, such as woodchips.

THE PROMISE OF BIOCHAR

A technology that's been gaining a lot of traction lately for its potential to both sequester carbon and improve soil quality is biochar. Essentially high-tech charcoal that's been rebranded for our climate-conscious era, biochar is made by heating—rather than burning—biomass such as plant residue or manure in specialized kilns at moderate temperatures under low-oxygen conditions.

The process, known as pyrolysis, transforms about 50 percent of the carbon in the raw materials into solid biochar and the rest into valuable liquid and gaseous by-products, some of which can be used as biofuels. The fine-grained biochar can be added directly into soil, though some practitioners recommend composting it first to make it more water absorptive.

Research on biochar is really just getting started, but initial studies show that it can improve the structure and nutrient-retention capacity of soils. It has also been shown to enhance biological activities such as nitrogen fixation and the penetration of plant roots by beneficial mycorrhizal fungi, though the processes are not understood. Because it raises soil pH, it can also be used as a liming agent. Finally, since the carbon in biochar is in a mineralized form, it is highly resistant to decay, and may last in the soil for hundreds or even thousands of years—though exactly how long it resides in the soil is a matter of some debate.

If adding charcoal to your garden soil sounds a bit barmy, then consider the famous *terra preta do indio*, or "dark earth of the Indians," of Brazil's Amazon Basin. The *terra preta* are patches of deep, dark, fertile loam scattered through a region with very poor soil, and their origins have long remained a mystery. Recently, however, scientists learned that the soils are man-made, and that much of their fertility can be attributed to the addition of charcoal by native agricultural societies thousands of years before the arrival of Columbus.

As promising as biochar might be, it's unclear how widely the technology will be adopted by the farming and gardening communities. Much research remains to be done, including how best to apply biochar to the soil. It's porous and light, so unless it's incorporated into the soil, biochar may be prone to erosion. If this is the case, then biochar may not be compatible with no-till gardening and farming.

Use compost as an alternative to peat. Long considered an ideal amendment for garden soil, peat is a big no-no in the climate-friendly garden. More than half of the planet's soil carbon pool is sequestered in the peatlands of the Northern Hemisphere. Harvesting peat for fuel or horticultural use releases enormous amounts of carbon dioxide into the atmosphere while destroying habitat for wetland plants and animals. Homemade compost is an excellent substitute for peat and—if made properly—has a negative carbon footprint. Coir dust manufactured from coconut husk fiber is also a good recycled and renewable alternative to peat; however, because it's imported from Asia, it has embodied emissions related to shipping.

Minimize disturbance of soil. One of the most effective ways to turn your soil into a carbon sink is to do as little as you can to upset it. Churning the soil with a roto-tiller or vigorously digging with a spade are—like plowing—harmful to many soil organisms (especially beneficial fungi), damage soil structure, and accelerate the loss of stored carbon to the atmosphere. Turning the earth also reverses the natural layers in the soil, bringing infertile subsoil to the surface and burying organic matter underneath—depriving plant roots of nutrients and potentially causing drainage problems. Digging also brings buried weed seeds to the surface, where they are quite happy to germinate. Following are tips to minimize soil disturbance in the garden:

- Avoid working in the garden when the soil is very wet or dry, because you can damage the soil structure.
- Grow mainly perennial plants, including trees and shrubs—once planted and established, perennials require little if any maintenance beyond an annual application of organic mulch; growing annuals generally requires more frequent perturbation of the soil.
- Keep bare soil covered with organic mulch, a dense groundcover, or cover crops to protect against the erosive forces of rain and wind.
- Install pavers or stepping-stones in the garden and planting beds to direct foot traffic and lessen its adverse impacts on soil.
- Switch to no-till and no-dig practices (see page 91).

Pavers or stepping-stones are handsome additions to the garden and help protect the soil by minimizing compaction.

Allow leaves and other plant residues to decompose. As much as is aesthetically tolerable, allow fallen leaves, grass clippings, and other plant residues to decompose naturally, and enrich the soil with nutrients and organic matter. If you prefer a tidy garden, you can opt to compost all your clippings and return the carbon and nutrients in the form of a compost mulch.

Spread organic mulch. The benefits of a thick layer of organic mulch in the garden are manifold: It suppresses weeds, conserves water, insulates plant roots from extremes of temperature, protects the soil against erosion caused by wind and rain, provides a source of slow-release nutrients to plants, and serves up a tasty meal for the fauna of the soil food web. Did I leave anything out? Oh, yes, it also helps build carbon levels in the soil.

Choices for organic mulches abound, but locally sourced recycled materials such as homemade compost, shredded leaves, and arborist wood chips are the most desirable from a carbon-counting perspective. Organic mulches are generally applied on garden beds and around woody plants at a depth of two to four inches, depending on such factors as soil texture, regional climate, and type of material, and need to be renewed once every year or two.

Grow nitrogen-fixing plants. Some plants engage in symbiotic relationships with soil bacteria that allow them to pull nitrogen out of the air and turn it into usable

mineral forms. Nitrogen-fixing clovers and legumes are commonly grown in many home vegetable gardens and make excellent winter cover crops—protecting bare ground from erosion, enriching the soil with nitrogen, preventing other nutrients from leaching out, and providing a source of organic matter when tilled under or mowed at the beginning of the planting season.

Nitrogen fixers can also provide valuable services in more ornamental areas of the garden. For instance, leguminous trees such as honey locust (*Gleditsia triacanthos*) and American yellowwood (*Cladrastis*

Bayberry, shown here in winter, is just one shrub that fixes nitrogen in the soil.

Drip-irrigation systems and soaker hoses release water slowly. This avoids puddling and related carbon loss through soil erosion.

kentukea) can naturally enrich the surrounding garden soil and reduce the need for energy-sapping inputs. As a bonus, growing nitrogen-fixing trees may also enhance soil carbon storage: Research has shown that forests with nitrogen-fixing trees accumulate more carbon than those that don't have any. No room in the garden to plant a tree? Not to worry! Many handsome shrubs also fix nitrogen, including northern bayberry (*Morella pensylvanica*), silver buffaloberry (*Shepherdia argentea*), and New Jersey tea (*Ceanothus americanus*).

The No-Till Approach

You may already be familiar with the concept of no-till gardening. Popular books such as Patricia Lanza's *Lasagna Gardening* have helped disseminate the idea to a mass audience. It may be an idea as old as agriculture itself, developed in an era when there were no plows around to churn the earth. However, the modern incarnation of no-till methods began after the development of alternative tillage tools such as the disk plow in the 1950s. Since then, a growing portion of the farming community in the United States has been shifting away from conventional tillage to more conservation-minded reduced-till or no-till approaches. Today, about 20 percent of our farmland is managed using no-till methods.

What are these exactly? Instead of vigorously plowing the soil to loosen clods and remove weeds, mix in amendments, and prepare seedbeds, no-till farmers take a less energy-intensive route—leaving plant roots and other residues untouched in the soil after harvest as a protective mulch layer, spraying herbicide

Minimal disturbance is key to carbon sequestration in soil. No-till techniques that have been evolving in large-scale farming since the 1950s are being adopted increasingly by gardeners.

to kill weeds prior to planting, and sowing directly into the unplowed earth using specialized machinery.

Organic no-till techniques have also been developed for large-scale farming, though as of yet they are not widely used. Practitioners of organic no-till methods steer clear of chemical herbicides and instead use cover crops to suppress weeds. Prior to planting their cash crops, they mechanically kill (that is, squish) the cover crops using large rollers and then sow directly into the green mulch. However, this organic system isn't strictly no-till because one round of tillage is required to sow the cover crops. Small-scale organic farmers have more options. For instance, they can use tarps to cover weed seedlings for a few weeks, weakening or killing them prior to direct planting in the soil.

No-till farming offers numerous benefits compared with plow-based agriculture. The permanent layer of plant residue resulting from no-till methods shields the soil from erosion, protects soil fauna, increases aggregation, enhances water infiltration, and reduces water loss from evaporation. No-till farming requires less use of machinery and so helps cut embodied carbon costs and fuel emissions. Many studies have demonstrated that not tilling also results in higher soil organic carbon sequestration than plow-based farming. However, a recent paper coauthored by Ohio State University's Rattan Lal raises some questions, suggesting that the carbon concentrations seem to be different only in the upper layers of the soil, and that they are negligible when the entire soil profile is taken into account—most likely because plows can bury surface plant residues deep down in the soil. However, Lal says more research is needed, because it is possible that the residence time of carbon in no-till soils is higher than in plowed soils.

Creating a No-Till Garden

It didn't take too long for gardeners to adapt ideas and transfer technology from the no-till farm movement to their backyards. Several influential books have appeared since the 1950s (see "For More Information," page 110) repackaging no-till farming as "no dig," "no work," and "no weed" gardening—with a little "no kidding" thrown in for good measure. The particulars of no-till gardening can vary significantly among practitioners, but the fundamental methodology is the same— dispense with digging as much as possible because it damages the soil, and use organic mulches to control weeds, prepare planting beds, and feed the soil organisms that nourish your plants.

Of course, most gardeners already practice a form of no-till horticulture in a portion of their yards, which is generally devoted to permanent plantings of trees, shrubs, and perennials. And it's already common knowledge that a yearly application of organic mulch is the best way to maintain established woody plants and mixed borders. Moreover, most gardeners are aware that digging in the soil around established plants risks damaging their feeder roots, which are located just below the soil surface. That said, the practice of preparing a new planting bed using the no-till method is starkly different from what most gardeners are accustomed to. Here

Year-round maintenance of a no-till garden involves renewing the mulch and carefully removing any weeds that manage to colonize the bed.

are the basic steps, summarized from writer and soil scientist Lee Reich's eminently practical *Weedless Gardening*:

1. Mow any existing vegetation as low as you can go.

2. Lay down a blanket of newspaper, four sheets thick, over the site of the new bed to kill what's left of the underlying vegetation.

3. Make sure to overlap the newspaper so there are no holes that plants can resprout through.

4. Wet the newspaper to keep it in place.

5. Apply a one- to three-inch-thick layer of weed-free mulch, such as compost or wood chips, on top of the newspaper (some no-till gardeners advocate much deeper sheet layering of mulch).

6. Wait a week or so before planting seedlings or sowing seeds directly into the mulch.

For planting into established beds, you can minimize soil disturbance by transplanting young, small plants, and preparing the planting holes with a bulb planter or dibble rather than a spade. Year-round maintenance mainly consists of removing any weeds that may colonize the bed, being careful not to drag out too much soil along with the weed roots (Reich recommends precision-cutting weeds out of the soil with a knife), and regularly renewing your mulch.

To create a no-till planting, lay down a blanket of newspaper, apply a generous layer of weed-free organic mulch, and plant seeds or seedlings directly in the mulch a week or so later.

Carbon comprises on average almost half of a plant's dry matter. Trees, both living and processed as wood products, sequester significant amounts of this element.

Carbon Sequestration in Plants

Plants fix carbon from the atmosphere through the biochemical process of photosynthesis. Mobilizing the green pigment chlorophyll in their leaves, they capture energy from sunlight and combine it with carbon dioxide (absorbed from the air through leaf pores) and water (taken up from the soil) to make simple sugars and oxygen, which is released as a byproduct into the air. Plants use the sugars to create new tissues, form complex molecules such as proteins for regulating metabolism, and as a source of energy to drive their metabolic activities.

Plant sugars form the building blocks of all sorts of very useful polymers, including cellulose, the main structural component of plant cell walls, and the large, complex molecule lignin, which confers mechanical strength to cell walls and is a principal component of wood. Carbon is the backbone of all these compounds. On average, it comprises just under half of a plant's dry matter.

When plants respire, breaking down the sugars they create during photosynthesis in the presence of oxygen to produce energy, they release carbon dioxide back into the atmosphere. However, the amount of CO_2 taken up by photosynthesis is generally far greater than that lost to respiration—and this results in a large net gain of carbon by plants in their tissues over the course of their lifetimes. As explained in the preceding section on soil, most of this carbon is eventually returned to the atmosphere when plants die and decompose.

Trees and Shrubs Are Key

In arid climates, long-lived agaves and cacti store carbon quite efficiently.

Plant species vary in their ability to accumulate and store carbon. Because they can grow to be quite large and live a relatively long time, woody plants—especially trees—are the champions of biotic carbon sequestration. The world's forests are enormous carbon sinks, and their continued destruction, especially in developing countries, to produce firewood and clear land for agriculture is a major source of global carbon emissions. According to the Earth Policy Institute, tropical deforestation causes the release of 2.2 billion tons of carbon per year.

Most of the serious discussions pertaining to large-scale carbon sequestration by plants center on growing lots and lots of trees, either by replanting them on land recently cleared of forest by timber harvesting or natural disaster (reforestation) or by planting new forests on land that has long been cleared of primary forest—such as agricultural fields and urban areas—or that has never been home to any trees (afforestation). One study estimates that if we halt clear-cutting of primary forest in the tropics and plant about two billion acres of trees in temperate and tropical zones, we can offset about a quarter of our current annual CO_2 emissions. (Planting trees in snowfields of boreal regions may not be a good idea, however; some research suggests that replacing light-reflecting expanses of snow cover with relatively dark and light-absorptive trees could actually accelerate global warming.)

Prairie Plants and Other Perennials

Gardeners can contribute to this big-picture sequestration project by planting and caring for trees and understory plants in their yards. Of course, growing any kind of plant will lead to some degree of temporary carbon storage, and gardeners can look elsewhere in nature besides forests for inspiration. Prairies and wetlands are highly productive ecosystems that are very adept at sequestering carbon in soil, and they may make more appropriate models for gardens in some locations. In arid climates, large, long-lived succulent plants such as certain cacti and agaves are very efficient at storing carbon.

Whatever you plant, the important thing to remember is to grow it in a sustainable way that minimizes the need for inputs such as fertilizer, pesticides, and supple-

URBAN FORESTS AND CARBON CAPTURE

Trees in cities and towns provide many ecological and human health services, from intercepting airborne pollutants to absorbing storm-water runoff. Urban forests can also play a critical role in our struggle to prevent climate change. Urban trees capture carbon dioxide directly from the air and sequester it in their leaves, branches, trunks, and roots. By shading buildings, streets, and parking lots and transpiring water from the soil into the air, they also reduce CO_2 levels indirectly—cooling cities in the summer and thus reducing energy consumption and fossil fuel emissions.

Urban areas currently occupy about 3.5 percent of the land base in the continental United States, and about 27 percent of this urban land area is covered by trees. In 2002, U.S. Forest Service researchers David Nowak and Daniel Crane calculated that urban trees in the lower 48 states store approximately 700 million tons of carbon and sequester it at a rate of 22.8 million tons a year. New York City's park, street, and garden trees make up the largest urban forest sink in the country—storing a total of more than 1.2 million tons of carbon.

Preserving and expanding our urban forests are important priorities. However, rapid urbanization and inadequate funding of city parks has led to a 30 percent decline in urban tree cover since the 1970s, according to the nonprofit conservation organization American Forests. Some cities have recently launched major tree-planting campaigns to rectify the problem. New York City and Los Angeles have each adopted ambitious initiatives to plant a million trees over the next decade. As gardeners, we can take action ourselves by planting trees in our yards and encouraging our communities to grow more trees in public spaces.

Urban trees like these in New York's Central Park capture and store carbon directly. By cooling the city, they also help save energy and reduce CO_2 emissions indirectly.

mental irrigation, all of which have large carbon footprints. This involves choosing climate- and site-appropriate species that require little if any maintenance once established. It generally doesn't involve having a big lawn, which for the vast majority of homeowners, will never be a carbon-neutral proposition (see page 36).

The Best Woody Plants

For most of us, growing trees and shrubs is by far the simplest way to sequester significant amounts of plant-based carbon in our gardens over the long term. Growing pretty much any woody plant—as long as it's hardy to your area, adapted to the environmental conditions of your garden, and disease resistant—will help draw down carbon dioxide levels in the air. Healthy trees sequester more carbon than stressed trees by growing more vigorously, requiring less maintenance, and living longer.

That said, some species are more efficient carbon sinks than others. Fast-growing trees, such as hybrid poplars and eucalypts, may seem like the best choice—and for plantation foresters interested in a quick method of both sequestering carbon and producing wood products (themselves, a form of stored carbon), they may well be. However, faster growers tend to have shorter life spans and accumulate less overall biomass than slower growers, such as walnut and hickory trees. For example, one study, carried out in Modesto, California, estimated that a common hackberry (*Celtis occidentalis*), which has a moderate growth rate, sequestered about five tons of carbon dioxide over 100 years, compared with a rapid-growing crape myrtle

(*Lagerstroemia indica*), which only managed to store about ⅛ ton of CO_2 in its relatively brief, 30-year life span.

Trees with denser wood also store more carbon. As a group, the "hardwoods," or flowering trees, tend on average to have denser wood than the "softwoods," or conifers. However, these descriptive categories, derived from the timber industry and commonly used in discussions about carbon offsets, can be misleading, because a lot of softwoods, such as larches, yews, and many of the pines, have very dense wood, and quite a number of hardwoods, such as alders, poplars, and some cherries, have relatively soft

Short-lived trees like poplars accumulate less carbon overall than long-lived species.

Newly planted trees sequester more carbon than older trees. However, old trees are valuable pools of stored carbon and important habitat for birds and other wildlife.

wood. Balsa (*Ochroma pyramidale*), a so-called hardwood, is so soft that you can indent it with your fingernail!

Newly planted trees sequester more carbon than older trees. As trees age, the rate at which they store carbon decreases. Very old trees may even release as much carbon dioxide through decay as they absorb through photosynthesis. However, old trees are valuable pools of stored carbon, and if they don't present a hazard to your home, they should be preserved as long as possible. Old and dead trees also serve as valuable habitat for wildlife such as insects and birds. If you remove a dying or dead tree from your garden, be sure to plant a new one right away to maintain the overall population in the landscape and compensate for the temporary loss of carbon from your personal pool. Using a dead tree to create wood-chip mulch or a piece of furniture—as opposed to burning it for firewood—results in further carbon storage; however, the greenhouse gas emissions associated with operating saws, chippers, or power tools need to be taken into account.

Calculating Carbon in Garden Trees

The U.S. Forest Service has developed two free computer programs that allow users to calculate how much carbon is stored in trees on their property—the Tree Carbon Calculator (TCC) and iTree (see "For More Information," page 110). Developed by Greg MacPherson and his colleagues at the Center for Urban Forest Research, the TCC provides quick carbon-storage calculations for 20 of the most predominantly

The best trees for carbon sequestration vary by region. Eastern white pine is on the list of tough, long-lived trees recommended by scientists for the area surrounding Syracuse, New York.

planted trees in 16 different reference cities around the United States. The iTree application is more comprehensive and complex and is based on many years of Forest Service research. Carbon estimates from both programs vary based on tree species, tree size, and regional climate.

Both tools can also calculate the amount of energy savings provided by trees planted around your home for shade and shelter. Strategic planting of trees and shrubs can save a great deal of energy (see "Landscaping for Home Energy Conservation," page 61), and the emissions reduction associated with these savings is likely much more significant—and permanent—than the carbon sequestered by the plants. After all, the average tree sequesters about a ton of carbon over its lifetime, which is just five percent of an average American's annual CO_2 emissions.

Based on their tree calculator data, MacPherson and his colleagues are developing lists of "best trees" for carbon sequestration in different U.S. regions. Other researchers are working on this as well. In 2007, scientists at SUNY College of Environmental Science and Forestry, in Syracuse, New York, developed a list of 31 recommended trees that, if planted together within that city's urban forest matrix, could double the current forest's ability to sequester carbon. The list is made up of a diverse mix of tough, long-lived, and mostly native species, including American basswood (*Tilia americana*), eastern white pine (*Pinus strobus*), red hickory (*Carya ovalis*), and gray birch (*Betula populifolia*). The plants were also chosen on the basis of being low emitters of volatile organic compounds, which can exacerbate air pollution in urban areas.

Constraints and Caveats

In general, you can't go wrong by adding more plants to your garden. Along with sequestering carbon and (if you plant trees and shrubs for screening and shade) reducing energy use in the home, plants provide a host of co-benefits, including increased biodiversity, habitat for wildlife, reduced air pollution, enhanced water infiltration, lower air temperature (due to transpiration), reduced soil erosion, and beautiful scenery. As with sequestration of carbon in the soil, however, the effects are temporary; gardeners must continue to replace their dead or diseased plants and preserve a consistent level of biomass in order to create a permanent sink.

Moreover, certain activities—in particular, maintenance practices that rely on the use of fossil-fuel-powered equipment—offset carbon gains from plant growth by releasing CO_2 into the atmosphere. Gardeners can minimize these emissions by using hand-powered tools whenever possible and by growing climate- and site-appropriate plant species that require little if any maintenance once established. Not all maintenance activities are bad, however! Plant-care techniques that extend the life span of your trees, shrubs, and perennials—such as watering tree transplants during the first year of establishment—can result in enhanced carbon storage in your garden.

QUICK TIPS FOR MAXIMIZING CARBON STORAGE IN YOUR PLANTS

The following tips for increasing carbon sequestration in your garden using vegetation are derived from design and management guidelines developed by the U.S. Forest Service's Center for Urban Forest Research, as well as other sources.

- Plant more trees and shrubs where feasible.
- Choose large (at maturity), long-lived species with dense wood.
- Extend the life of your plants (and thus the duration of carbon storage) by growing regionally hardy and site-appropriate species and practicing sustainable plant care.
- Grow tough, adaptable native plants.
- Avoid high-maintenance or disease-susceptible species.
- Plant a diverse mix of trees, shrubs, and perennials (biodiverse gardens are healthier and more resilient).
- Provide your trees and shrubs with enough room (above- and below-ground) to grow to full maturity.
- Grow a mix of species of different ages and sizes to ensure a continuous canopy and understory over time.
- Replace any trees and shrubs removed due to old age, wind damage, or disease.
- Don't forget to mulch!

Beyond the Garden
Barbara Pearson

Maybe you've planted all the trees and shrubs your property can hold, stopped using chemical fertilizers, have a compost pile, and are feeling justifiably proud of your garden's climate footprint. Still, you find yourself thinking that there must be more you can do. There is! You can participate in any number of local and national initiatives to complement the effort you put into maintaining a climate-conscious garden.

Many of the initiatives don't sequester carbon or reduce carbon footprints by planting anything, so you don't even have to get your hands dirty. Some focus on providing data for climate change research. Others ensure that healthy food does not go to waste.

Besides scratching your itch to do more, there's plenty in it for you. You can hone your observational skills and network with like-minded people. Some projects provide a bit of training, so there's a chance you'll learn something new. Many provide opportunities for people who don't have their own gardens, or don't actually like to garden. This chapter provides snapshots of just a few of the many important initiatives going on now.

Citizen Science

Citizen science has been practiced for centuries; some say that it can be traced back to at least Galileo; others cite Archimedes in the second century BCE. Many scientists put a very high value on the work of volunteers, who collect vast amounts of data. Some are convinced that information collected by citizen scientists is unbeatable for its accuracy, scope, and extraordinary price (free).

Current projects can be located on Cornell University's Citizen Science Central website (birds.cornell.edu/citscitoolkit/projects/find), where you can browse by categories such as Climate Change or Plants. Local and national projects are listed, each with a description of the project's goals and geographic scope. Universities and Cooperative Extension offices are additional sources of information on citizen science projects that are locally based.

Mountain Watch Plant Monitoring Program
outdoors.org/conservation/mountainwatch
This project of the Appalachian Mountain Club recruits hikers to become citizen scientists and collect data for studies of alpine and forest plants along hiking trails. Volunteers may opt for various levels of participation, from spending a few minutes checking plants at trail junctions or mountain peaks to a longer-term commitment to observe a particular location over time. Observations are entered online and support a long-term study of how shifts in climate trends impact mountain flora.

Community food projects and planting trees in your town or city offer ways to go beyond the garden to help ameliorate climate change.

usanpn.org/?q=content/lilachoneysuckle-program

For over 50 years, volunteers across the United States and Canada have collected phenological observations of the lilac cultivar *Syringa chinensis* 'Red Rothomagensis' as part of the University of Wisconsin-Milwaukee's Indicator Observation Program (now administered by the National Phenology Network). Cloned plants (genetically identical individuals) are used to help minimize response variations between locations. Participants plant, grow, and observe the lilac's bloom time and other phenological events over many years. The resulting data has been used to assess the general impact of climate change on the onset of spring in North America.

Tree-Planting Initiatives

In addition to sequestering carbon, trees offer many other environmental benefits, such as reducing airborne pollutants, mitigating storm-water runoff, and lowering temperatures in summer. Trees can provide cities with economic benefits in excess of five times the cost of planting and maintaining them, so it's no surprise that any internet search for "million trees" will find tree-planting initiatives in most large cities.

Simply planting trees is not enough. Young trees are particularly fragile in urban environments and require careful attention to their watering and other cultivation needs—as well as protection from the hazards of trucks, salt, and pets. (In Los Angeles in 2007, the mortality rate of newly planted trees was over 40 percent.) Tree steward-

Tree-planting projects are now under way in most large cities and on every continent except frozen Antarctica. Above, volunteers in Mexico prepare seedlings for planting.

SNAPSHOT: PROJECT BUDBURST

budburst.org

Goal This project aims to engage citizen scientists across the country in collecting climate change data based on leafing and flowering times of trees and other plants.

Project Manager The National Corporation for Atmospheric Research administers the project in partnership with the Chicago Botanic Garden and the College of Forestry and Conservation of the University of Montana.

How to Participate Register online, download the project workbook, select a local plant to monitor, and report your observations.

Description Becoming involved in this project could be a participant's first awareness of phenology, the study of the timing of life-cycle events in plants (and animals) as they relate to climatic conditions. The first unfurling of leaves, first flower opening, and first ripe fruit are all biological events in plants, called phenophases, that are affected by factors such as day length, temperature, and precipitation, the latter two being of special concern in global climate change. Volunteers can choose plants to monitor from a list of 75 easily identified and widespread candidates (but may monitor and report on any plant to which they have access). The Budburst website provides a tool for determining the latitude and longitude of the location of observed plants.

All reporting is done via Project Budburst's website, either as observations are made (preferred) or in one account at the end of the season. While you are free to participate to any extent you want, daily observations are preferred, and making observations of as many phenophases as possible is most helpful. The project also displays results as they are available. Information on the 100 most recently reported observations, some including photos, can be viewed online, and data from the project's previous years can be downloaded in several formats.

Accomplishments In 2008, almost 5,000 observations were reported from participants in 49 states, creating a baseline set of data.

ship programs train citizens how to care for the trees in their community. Alliance for Community Trees offers an extensive list, by state, of tree organizations involved in the planting, care, and promotion of urban trees (actrees.org/site/aboutus).

MillionTreesNYC

milliontreesnyc.org

Begun in October 2007, MillionTreesNYC (MTNYC) involves public and private efforts to achieve three main goals: getting one million new trees planted in the city, ensuring that those young trees get the care they need to become established, and offering training in arboriculture, ecological and garden restoration, and design. The New York Restoration Project works with MTNYC to find places on public

SNAPSHOT: TREEPEOPLE/MILLION TREES LA

treepeople.org

Goal TreePeople's mission is to inspire, engage, and support people to take personal responsibility for the urban environment—making it safe, healthy, fun, and sustainable—and to share the results as a model for the world.

Project Manager TreePeople, an environmental nonprofit, runs the project along with the Los Angeles Department of Recreation and Parks for Million Trees LA.

How to Participate Volunteer online for any of numerous community programs that include tree planting, tree care, mountain restoration, reforestation, park maintenance, seedling care, and community outreach in the Los Angeles area.

Description TreePeople was founded in 1973 by Andy Lipkis, who was 17 at the time and had just successfully raised $10,000 to plant sugar pines at local summer camps. The Million Trees LA initiative is one of many projects that further TreePeople's goal of developing a "functioning community forest" in every neighborhood in the city. To that end, TreePeople organizes and manages an extensive set of programs. The Citizen Forester Program provides resources and free citizen forester training for community tree planting and care. The Fruit Tree Program establishes free fruit trees in low-income communities. Repairing wildfire devastation to the forests surrounding the city is the work of Forest Aid and the California Wildfire Restoration Initiative.

Environmental education programs for schools, youth groups, and teachers; free bimonthly community greening workshops; and tree pruning and pest management workshops make the list of services TreePeople provides seemingly endless. A visit to its website is an education in itself: Extensive information on tree planting and care, rainwater capture methods, pest alerts from government agencies, and a glossary are available to anyone who's interested. The organization's headquarters in Coldwater Canyon Park are open to the public and house the Center for Community Forestry.

Accomplishments Los Angeles's first Million Tree Campaign planted one million trees before the 1984 Summer Olympics. More than 80,000 fruit trees have been distributed in the city's neighborhoods, and 20,050 tree seedlings were planted in the San Bernardino National Forest after the 2003 wildfires.

and private property that could use more trees. The MTNYC Stewardship Corps relies on the expertise of Brooklyn Botanic Garden and Trees New York to provide tree-care workshops and citizen pruner training. The contributions of private and philanthropic entities are also an essential element of the city's greening plans.

Philadelphia Orchard Project

phillyorchards.org

Community-based groups and volunteers plant orchards in vacant lots, community gardens, and schoolyards in Philadelphia's neediest neighborhoods.

Food-rescue projects not only help provide fruits and vegetables for the needy but also reduce carbon emissions by eliminating waste.

Trees Forever

treesforever.org

For 20 years, Trees Forever has been planting trees in neighborhoods, on school grounds, and along highways in Iowa and Illinois. Volunteers engage in other activities as well, such as landscaping in business districts and caring for storm-damaged trees.

Trees, Water & People

treeswaterpeople.org

Projects include planting trees for windbreaks and shade as part of the Tribal Lands Renewable Energy program in Colorado, reforestation projects in Central and South America, and selling carbon offset that support tree-planting projects.

Food Rescue

Who would disagree that throwing away perfectly good food must end? Subordinate to the human issue that there are people who need food and don't have it, the environmental impact of producing food that never nourishes anyone is becoming a serious focus of efforts to reduce carbon emissions by eliminating waste. Food-rescue organizations take donations of food from private citizens, growers, wholesalers, and restaurants to help community kitchens and food pantries provide sustenance for the poor. Many are now more actively promoting their work as environmentally sound as well as humanitarian. Volunteers are always needed.

Cleveland Foodbank
clevelandfoodbank.org
More than 450 hunger centers throughout northeastern Ohio have received millions of pounds of food rescued by the Cleveland Foodbank.

Food Finders
foodfinders.org
Based in Long Beach, California, Food Finders has fed the hungry of Southern California since 1989 by, among other things, keeping over 72 million pounds of food out of the waste stream.

Forgotten Harvest
forgottenharvest.org
Forgotten Harvest's mission is to relieve hunger in the Detroit metropolitan community by rescuing prepared and perishable food and donating it to emergency food providers. It currently rescues 9.5 million pounds of food per year collected from grocery stores, restaurants, dairies, wholesalers, and others.

Portland Fruit Tree Project
portlandfruit.org
Fruit and nuts from trees in Portland, Oregon, are harvested by volunteers who donate half of the harvest to local food banks.

Seed Exchanges
Many seed-exchange groups encourage organic practices and the use of heirloom varieties as sustainability measures. Community seed swaps offer opportunities to share seeds and plants. They also provide a great way to meet like-minded neighbors and build community while supporting sustainable food choices.

iVillage GardenWeb Seed Exchange
forums2.gardenweb.com/forums/exseed/
This very active message board allows participants to list or locate seeds available for trade (no items are for sale).

Seed exchanges encourage organic practices and the use of heirloom varieties.

SNAPSHOT: BACKYARD HARVEST

backyardharvest.org

Goal Backyard Harvest uses food resources the community already has on hand to provide locally grown fresh produce to people in need via food banks, meal programs, senior centers, and other community organizations.

How to Participate Contact Backyard Harvest via its website or sign-up booths at local events and markets. Chapters currently exist in California, Idaho, and Minnesota, and there are plans for a national network. Local chapters can be formed with a user-friendly and low-cost licensing agreement and set of resources.

Description Backyard Harvest is a nonprofit organization begun in 2006 after its founder, Amy Grey, found herself with 200 heads of lettuce she hadn't planned on. Donating them to the local food bank was the "seed" for what became a series of community-based gathering, gleaning, and growing programs. Home gardeners can donate extra food or participate in Backyard Harvest's Grow More to Share More program, which provides seeds, plant starts, and compost to gardeners who grow excess food for donation. The Town Orchard program, created after an elderly woman with a fully loaded apple tree told Grey she could have them if she picked them, allows people to register their fruit trees or small orchards to be harvested.

In Idaho, the Palouse Gardening Collaborative brings together landowners not using their land or unable to keep up with their gardens and gardening novices willing to grow food for others while learning to grow for themselves. Each of these programs is supported by volunteers, with or without gardens of their own, who help harvest and deliver food and collect after-market produce from farmers' markets.

Accomplishments During the organization's first three years, over 150,000 pounds of fresh food have been provided to thousands of families in need.

Seed Ambassadors Project

seedambassadors.org

Based in Oregon, this nonprofit seed-stewardship initiative promotes the sharing of open-pollinated, locally adapted seed; increases regional food security through biodiversity of food crops; and promotes organic practices in the production of seed.

Seed Savers Exchange

seedsavers.org

Seed Savers Exchange is a nonprofit organization of gardeners dedicated to saving and sharing heirloom seeds and is the largest nongovernmental seed bank in the United States. An active forum allows participants to swap seeds and plant starts and share information about vegetable growing.

For More Information

GARDENING RESOURCES

*Regenerative Organic Farming:
A Solution to Global Warming*
Tim LaSalle and Paul Hepperly, Rodale
Institute, 2008

Royal Horticultural Society Guide to
Gardening in a Changing Climate
rhs.org.uk/climate

Landscaping Choices

Sustainable Sites Initiative
www.sustainablesites.org
Rating system and case studies for
sustainable landscapes

U.S. Department of Energy
www.energysavers.gov/your_home/
landscaping/index.cfm/mytopic=11910
Resources on landscaping for energy
efficiency

U.S. Forest Service Center for
Urban Forest Research
www.fs.fed.us/psw/programs/cufr/tree_
guides.php
Information on tree placement, tree
selection, and other practices to maximize
energy savings

Lawn Alternatives

*Easy Lawns: Low-Maintenance
Native Grasses for Gardeners
Everywhere*
Stevie Daniels, editor, Brooklyn Botanic
Garden, 2001

Eco-Lawn
www.eco-lawn.com

Grass Roots Program
www.grassrootsprogram.com
Grass climate footprint calculator

*Redesigning the American Lawn:
A Search for Environmental Harmony*
F. Herbert Bormann, Diana Balmori, and
Gordon T. Geballe, Yale University Press,
second edition, 2001

Healthy Soil

Easy Compost
Beth Hanson, editor, Brooklyn Botanic
Garden, 2001

*Healthy Soils for
Sustainable Gardens*
Niall Dunne, editor, Brooklyn Botanic
Garden, 2009

International Biochar Initiative
biochar-international.org

No-Till Gardening

Gardening Without Work
Ruth Stout, Cornerstone Library, 1975

Lasagna Gardening
Patricia Lanza, Rodale Books, 1998

No-Dig, No-Weed Gardening
Raymond P. Poincelot, Rodale Press, 1986

*Organic Gardening: The Natural
No-Dig Way*
Charles Dowding, Green Books, 2007

Weedless Gardening
Lee Reich, Workman Publishing, 2001

Water Conservation

Rainwater HOG
rainwaterhog.com
Modular tank system

WaterSense
www.epa.gov/watersense
Water-use calculators and conservation
information

CLIMATE CHANGE RESEARCH AND ADVOCACY

350.org
www.350.org/about/science
Movement to make 350 ppm the global target for carbon dioxide emissions

Botanic Gardens Conservation International Climate Change Centre
bgci.org/climate
Information about climate change, including *Plants and Climate Change: Which Future* report

Intergovernmental Panel on Climate Change
www.ipcc.ch
Includes the *Fourth Assessment Report*, released in 2007

Pew Center on Global Climate Change
pewclimate.org
Reports, fact sheets, and other resources on the science and economics of climate change

Post Carbon Institute
www.postcarbon.org
Ideas and models for transitioning from the carbon-addicted world to the post-carbon world

U.S. EPA Climate Change Website
epa.gov/climatechange

U.S. Forest Service Climate Change Primer
www.fs.fed.us/ccrc/primers/climate-change-primer.shtml

U.S. Global Change Research Program
globalchange.gov
Regional climate-change information and downloadable reports

ONLINE TOOLS AND CALCULATORS

Arbor Day Foundation Hardiness Zone Map
www.arborday.org/treeinfo/zonelookup.cfm

Build Carbon Neutral Construction Carbon Calculator
buildcarbonneutral.org

Climate Wizard
climatewizard.org
Allows users to create images, maps, and video of how the climate is changing in their cities, towns, and states

U.S. Forest Service i-Tree Software Suite
itreetools.org
Urban forestry analysis and benefits-assessment tools

Center for Urban Forest Research Tree Carbon Calculator
www.fs.fed.us/ccrc/topics/urban-forests
Windows-based software

SUSTAINABLE PRODUCTS

Forest Stewardship Council
www.fsc.org

Organic Materials Review Institute
www.omri.com

Recycled Content Product Directory
www.ciwmb.ca.gov.rcp

Sustainable Forestry Initiative
www.sfiprogram.org

U.S. EPA Environmentally Preferable Purchasing
www.epa.gov/epp
Information on green products, including online calculators

Veriflora
www.veriflora.com

Reuse, Recycle, and Exchange Programs

Earth911
www.earth911.com
Articles and information on recycling, including a database of recycling centers

Freecycle
www.freecycle.org

Industrial Material Exchange
www.govlink.org/hazwaste/business/imex

The Recyclers Exchange
www.recycle.net/exchange

Reuse Development Organization (RDO)
www.redo.org

Salvaged Building Materials Exchange
www.greenguide.com/exchange

SUSTAINABLE FOOD RESOURCES

American Community Gardening Association
www.communitygarden.org
Nonprofit membership organization of advocates for community gardening; website provides a directory of community gardens

Common Ground Organic Garden Supply and Education Center
www.commongroundinpaloalto.org
California-based nonprofit nursery offering organic gardening classes

Garden Organic: The National Charity for Organic Growing
www.gardenorganic.org.uk
The United Kingdom's "organic growing charity," whose website is a resource for organic gardeners

Seed Savers Exchange
www.seedsavers.org
Nonprofit organization that saves and shares heirloom seeds

Slow Food International
www.slowfood.com
A nonprofit, eco-gastronomic member-supported organization founded in 1989 to counteract fast food and fast life

Food Gardening Techniques

Edible Forest Gardens: The Ecology and Design of Home Scale Food Forests
Dave Jacke with Eric Toensmeier, Chelsea Green Publishing, 2005

Rodale's Illustrated Encyclopedia of Organic Gardening: The Complete Guide to Natural & Chemical-Free Gardening
Pauline Pears, editor, Dorling Kindersley, 2005

Roses Love Garlic: Companion Planting and Other Secrets of Flowers
Louise Riotte, Storey Publishing, 1998

Saving Seeds: The Gardener's Guide to Growing and Storing Vegetable and Flower Seeds
Marc Rogers, Storey Publishing, 1990

Seed to Seed: Seed Saving and Growing Techniques for Vegetable Gardeners
Suzanne Ashworth, Seed Savers Exchange, 2002

Contributors

Janet Marinelli, former director of publishing at Brooklyn Botanic Garden, is the author of several books on plants, gardening, and sustainable design, including *Plant*, a unique global reference featuring 2,000 species around the world that are threatened with extinction in their native habitats but alive in horticulture. Janet has won numerous awards, including one from the American Horticultural Society for "making a significant contribution to horticulture." Her company, Blue Crocus Consulting (janetmarinelli.com), specializes in interpretation and publishing projects.

Niall Dunne is a former editor of Brooklyn Botanic Garden's *Plants & Gardens News* and *Urban Habitats*; he also edited the BBG handbooks *Great Natives for Tough Places* and *Healthy Soils for Sustainable Gardens*. He holds an MA in English from University College Dublin and an MS in ecology and evolution from Rutgers University. He lives in Seattle and manages publications for the Arboretum Foundation at Washington Park Arboretum.

Amanda Knaul studied horticulture at the New York Botanical Garden and is currently working in the herbarium of Brooklyn Botanic Garden. Amanda is a local food enthusiast with a passion for all things green. She is also writing her first novel.

Kelly Ogrodnik is the sustainable design and programs manager at Phipps Conservatory in Pittsburgh. She manages the development and implementation of environmentally sustainable operations on the Phipps campus and serves as a reference source to the public and the international green community. Kelly holds an MLA degree from Chatham University and a BA from Pennsylvania State University in environmental and renewable resource economics.

Barbara Pearson is a graduate of the School of Professional Horticulture at the New York Botanical Garden. Her love of tropical plants was her motivation for becoming the owner and head grower of the greenhouse in Brooklyn where she had shopped for many years. Barbara was a computer programmer before making horticulture her career.

Susan Pell is the molecular plant systematist and laboratory manager at Brooklyn Botanic Garden, where she oversees the laboratories and conducts research in floristics of the tropics and the molecular systematics, nomenclature, and taxonomy of the cashew family (Anacardiaceae). Her research includes field expeditions to Australia, Costa Rica, Gabon, Peru, Madagascar, and Papua New Guinea. She holds a PhD in plant biology from Louisiana State University.

Photos

Illustrations

Index

PROVIDING EXPERT GARDENING ADVICE FOR OVER 60 YEARS

Join Brooklyn Botanic Garden as an annual Subscriber Member and receive our award-winning gardening handbooks delivered directly to you, plus *Plants & Gardens News*, *BBG Members News*, and privileges at many botanic gardens across the country. Visit bbg.org/subscribe for details.

BROOKLYN BOTANIC GARDEN GUIDES

World renowned for pioneering gardening information, Brooklyn Botanic Garden's award-winning guides provide practical advice in a compact format for gardeners in every region of North America. To order other fine titles, call 718-623-7286 or shop online at bbg.org/handbooks. For more information about Brooklyn Botanic Garden, call 718-623-7200 or visit bbg.org.